NEXT DAY

NEXT DAY

NEW AND SELECTED
POEMS

Cynthia Zarin

ALFRED A. KNOPF
NEW YORK
2024

THIS IS A BORZOI BOOK PUBLISHED
BY ALFRED A. KNOPF

Copyright © 2024 by Cynthia Zarin

aaknopf.com

Portions of this work originally collected in the following publications:
The Swordfish Tooth (Alfred A. Knopf, 1989); *Fire Lyric* (Alfred A. Knopf,
1993); *The Watercourse* (Alfred A. Knopf, 2002); *The Ada Poems* (Alfred
A. Knopf, 2010); *Orbit* (Alfred A. Knopf, 2017).

Pages 243 and 245 constitute an extension of this copyright page.

LIBRARY OF CONGRESS CATALOGING-IN-PUBLICATION DATA
Name: Zarin, Cynthia, author.
Title: Next day : new & selected poems / Cynthia Zarin.
Description: First edition. | New York : Alfred A. Knopf, 2024.
Identifiers: LCCN 2023037015 (print) | LCCN 2023037016 (ebook) |
ISBN 9780593536155 (hardcover) | ISBN 9780593536162 (ebook)
Subjects: LCGFT: Poetry.
Classification: LCC PS3576.A69 N49 2024 (print) |
LCC PS3576.A69 (ebook) | DDC 811/.54—dc23
LC record available at https://lccn.loc.gov/2023037015
LC ebook record available at https://lccn.loc.gov/2023037016

Front-of-jacket art: *Pamet River* by Rose Seccareccia
Jacket design by John Gall

Manufactured in the United States of America
First Edition

For Deborah Garrison

Contents

THE WATERCOURSE

(2002)

THE ADA POEMS

(2010)

ORBIT

(2017)

NEXT DAY: NEW POEMS

from

THE SWORDFISH TOOTH

(1989)

The Orchard Dialogue

The wings of what you think
open over the tin roofs, up where
the milkweed grows and two songs,

here, and then, converge.
The tune disappears. The stars
are small as bluebells

and distant as childhood. The streets
repeat themselves, each
one a boardwalk, with its circle

of pretty girls. *"Oh give me
all there is to love,"* she sang.
The man who ran the gramophone

under the makeshift bandstand
is gone. And in the corner
of the orchard, the peach

tree flutters a few leaves
in the silvery darkness.
Out on the veranda, a girl

lights the Japanese lanterns,
and her reflection, cast back to you
by her own taper, pleats on the water.

She wavers on the pond's slight current
like a broken oar. The dory rocks,
empty in the shallows, and it's

as if you, dimly yourself, must row
the next minutes, even hours,
towards some histrionic conclusion.

But, impossibly, you can't remember
even simple facts: orchard, pond, street—
girl. Between the pond and

the veranda, the mulberries flower
paper-thin, fragrant as the songs
sung under the arbor. The mind

balks. The view is a history
of recitations, place-names
and their colors: it is autumn—

she is a field above
the tree line, the valley gone
to seed and riot.

The Moon and the River Bank

The moon with its scalloped curve
and paper oceans: we've never been there.
The sky is a gap in the river
where the treelight clears, and the moon
is an old memento, a glass dome
where it snows on the village,

the sky full of little cloudy stars.
This is the shape the earth makes;
the reef, with its lapidary charm
records each jewel in the beadwork
of hot afternoons, and broached, the days
are all thoughtless, all memory, retrograde.
Now, restive, figured with the bird cries

and clicks, the children loiter
on the river bank; their shouts turning another wheel
into the yellow glow. But daylight
plays itself out, and hopeful,
contradictory, the effort lags in its mottled wake,
as if it could find a channel other

than this river in the heart,
a tributary with its banks cleared
of broken trees and bottles. But the moon
shows only where the willow
tricks the current. See how its face
is scrawled with leaves? The continents,
dim barges, drag on their water.

Fugue: Down at the Lake

Down at the lake, the grass is broken
where the boats were hauled aground.

                    That was
this morning, and afterwards, we swam out
to where the cold is deepest, and
there is only sky, unrimmed by trees.

                    A car passes
on the ridge behind the house. Tonight,
your voice, rising, falling, is so phrased
it could be music.

                    The tall grass ripples
around the old pilings, and above, over
the green-black night, the moon holds summer
like a gaze.

                    The day started early,
we hauled the boats up on to the shore.
Now, lingering, as I turn
to meet you, I hear only

                    the shrill clamor of insects:
the shape of the great, colloquial dark.

Looking for the Great Horned Owl in Truro Woods

The three of us went out
to look for owls,
and one of us knew how

to cup his hands, and make
an inquiring sound,
and, coaxed from behind the dunes,

there came an answering round.
There were two of them
that we could hear,

a muted, mating croon
that seemed to pulse
and find its echo

on the pond's curved lip.
And then, what was more mysterious
than us, crashing through the woods

to see a sound?

The Near and Dear

I   WHERE YOU ARE

Paris, and all the streets muffled,
the copper glare of windows, the click-click
over the drain grate. I can't be where
you are, the melodeon incessant
in the background, two students
sprawled like cats across the bar.
                              But in New York,
you are saying, and even your old clothes
seem to shine, mother-of-pearl
in the low-light, and I am kissing you,
kissing you good-bye.

II   ELSEWHERE

We take up residence, elsewhere.
Elsewhere, a packet boat
slow on the Potomac, shade
trees, mosquitoes bridling
in the scuppernong.
What was once a different country
resettles in the arbor—lamplight
pooling on the room's
plaited tail ends, times of day,
daylight clumping in the thorny hedges.

What was once, then, is:
column after column, the homestead
reflects in its own pond, where
house after house surfaces, then

drifts (one burned, one altered
by the sleeping porch, the shed)—
the family fortune, out rowing
in little boats.

The pond is full, tight net of
water lilies in the blade-thin hush.

Time gone, then, in the blade-thin hush.
In this little country of the soul,
another country curls into itself,
the house with its cornices, its
crenellations. And thought takes wing
to clear a wider space—landing,
falling in the garden.

III   THE PIGEONS

Stone lion by the gatehouse, and
all the pigeons, preening themselves.
Homing pigeons, you said, or doves,
the morning they blew to the window,
high over the duck pond, over the rosebushes.
Cooing in the ivy, and all the horrible ruckus,
I hated their dark wallow in the rafters.
Squawking barnacles, vertiginous—at noon
the black-clad friars fed their belching crowd,
acres of bread, gobble over the piazza.

IV   FABLE

A day catching blue marlin
in the warm bay—he told me about her
kiss, the shape of it, how he
could hear the sea in it.

Clams for supper,
a rotting set of Balzac
on the sleeping porch, girls and soldiers
in old *Life* magazines, their glassy
gray patina. Four thunderstorms
off the Chesapeake, smoke billowing
from a gigantic train—the house
was a cavern of dark and whitewashed rafters,
his sister's doll house took up
half the room.

V   COR CORDIUM

Keats's house, and all the paraphernalia
of journeys, midnight returns—two locks
of hair, fastened in a blue glass. It's all
so secretive, the narrow stair to the shrine,
the four versions of his body,
burning near the pine grove. You can go
to the pine grove, think of it,
the family jokes, the masquerades,
the sweetheart dogs and children
tight bundled in the carriage.

Think of it, the ride back—the scene
whizzes by, and you stare down at Florence,
flung like a brocade across the valley.
Imagine, then, the road to the villa
ending, and they open the door and you
break the news.

VI THE NEAR AND DEAR

Daily. Daily, the clouds lagging
over the marsh come faster, the sky
pushing behind them, and three days running
a compass point of birds, a chevron
marking time of day, then time of year.

Daylight, and far over the harbor
the vista with its flapping sails,
milk cans cluttering up the prow.
But wait, a house full of bells and calls,
a house with room after room
of trees: table, chairs, the bedpost carved
to look like a sapling. Ring after ring,
the bell is calling you to dinner
—to shape your napkin into a bird—
and I am calling you, calling out your name,
love like an aubade of bells,
a solitary ringing from the steeple.

Field Guide

The stars are pinned between the leaves
of the trees, and love is only a harbinger,
a regular Boy Scout handbook
of things not to do, and how to do other things,
small chores you'd never think of,
and supper gets cold on the table.
But I can't leave here without
taking you with me.
And the formal customs we once had,
like wearing red during hunting season,
are only signposts pointing the way
in and out of the territories—
colored leaves floating on the water,
hesitant, before the rains come.

Colophon

FOR OWEN ANDREWS

Rain of the months and years we had
known each other pressed in, printing
the new car as we left the wedding.
Larkspur, phlox, roses weedy in the
gravel, the stretch of slanted windows,
the meander of spring into summer
in the beanfield. The relief of going
hit in a peculiar way, abreast,
a spreading stain: the rain sloshed
on the windshield. As we went, the church
rose into the brink, and we counted out
the white dresses and the school ties,
the vows. The hillside spiraled,
chestnut, and along the service road
Lady Bird's florals glistened, so that
even now, speaking in the rain,
we think of her—her little hats,
triangular in the heartland.
Our glance lit on fenceposts, water
towers, the road frayed like a hymnal
ribbon as we followed it, winding
past the resort towns: Shelburne, Barrington,
Tanglewood, the misty profile of Brahms
in the treetops, under the striped tents.
Ahead of us, the rain came in ridges,
whole meadows of water, and the air
was matted: three centuries of water
since the bells pealed out. My shoes
were wet in the dew, waiting
for the ceremony, and now, looking
over towards you, I saw your face
cloudy against the dripping window.

. . .

Early in the morning, we stood on the lawn
and watched the boys playing kickball
against the scarred wall of the parsonage.
                    "Which one was you,"
I asked, "before the deluge?"

The Garnet Bracelet

I

In the ruined shoulder of a woodland
trail, that, one winter, a dwarf crane
on skis, a cursing Rumpelstiltskin,
enraged beyond all reason, it
took me an hour to get up,
    that now, in summer, seems a gentle

      ironic rise: two rocks, elephant
hides in liquid shade, drinking their
own thundering darkness, and, over
them, black raspberries broiling with
thorns, their black blood loosening in
    the rocks' topmost solarium; and

      my white arm a maypole wound with
ribbon scratches, reaching—again—
for the writhing branches: there,
you pointed, were the garnets. And
I looked, expecting a lapidary
    flash, a clawsfoot bijoued with

      red polish, crept out from under the
boulder's drenched side. But there were only
elderly gray stones, by the rotted
oak trunk's gaping maw, gothic as
the nobbed coif of a Scots gargoyle,
    each stone numb in the dry water-

      fall of its brethren, resistant,
holding in its warm wine: not to be

easily broken, like the nuptial
goblet, crushed underfoot beneath
a tassled awning, but, rather,
     each a complicit eye, weathered

     shut by unimaginable
sorrow, knowing that only mortal
injury—a merciless beating
of its rough hide in a tumbler,
then the mirroring, intrinsic
     scalpel—would let its dark heart gleam.

II

     A year later. The seasons closing
their court dance, and, high noon, on my
birthday, in our match of catch-as-
can, you tossed a garnet bracelet
in my lap, two flush rows of stones
     —dusk arbor with a gold latch—all

     the more precious for being less
dear, a gift shrugging at glamor,
the unnecessary rajah, but
nonetheless madly agleam, the
red lights blinking a faint code: sweetheart
     roses, restraint, tea; proportion's

     walled garden, its small vista, rather
than proposition. And garnets
being cold-weather stones, as you fastened
them around my summer wrist, they seemed
a vow for another autumn,
     the view laboriously improved

with mulched chrysanthemums—for who
could think a few posies would come
at such a cost—a vow that cheered
us, both still thoughtless as nurslings,
still bound at spleen, and mouth, and hip,
    each other's honing caresses

    placating, deft, so that neither you
nor I would have to wake; our doused
months, as I remember them, dully
glinting evenings, a medicinal
row of bottles; a grove of ninepins,
    tilting in a hollow—their clatter

    breaking the twinned sleep that finally
wore us down. And then everything, as
we would have put it, ordinary,
dreamt-of, happened: the pins,
left to their own devices, scattered,
    the blooms, untended in the garden,

III

    mouldering, the Mill iris bulbs
cataracts, withered with neglect,
June rounding June the green stalks
not blooming, turned to raffia,
and in the cheap jewelry box
    in the sock drawer where, carelessly,

    I keep it, the garnet bracelet
a red-rimmed cyclops eye gone blind from
weeping—that one word, *keep,* divorced
too from its romantic history;

the Old Norse "kopen," to stiffen,
     gape; and also you pretending,

     a joke under the plaid blankets
to be a bird caught in the brambles:
cheep, the long vowels beseeching—
the bracelet, since I will not wear it,
saved, there is no other explanation,
     for someone else, in the event,

     biding, of phantasmagorical
calamity—you dead, a . . . . . daughter?
—each claret garnet a separate
attempt at swallowing that once
stuck in my throat, pooling there
     to elemental darkness, and

     I turned to a stone elephant,
ornamental, guarding the runic
path of dumb happiness; the garnet
bracelet now a sleeping dervish,
precious because still left, that
     roused from its hollow in the chest

     would spin its fascinated circle
endlessly, a blood dance around
my wrist, and each stone a grief in
its setting of thorns would name its
roll-call of injuries, the prongs
tearing my skin, and the cuts burning.

His First Love Speaks

Do you remember, chick, my chickadee,
the silky day that rose, an otter swimming
toward winter, sleek and sure, the vanished slipper
of marriage, heel gone, in its faithful mouth?
So cold, the humping caterpillar house!
Cash churned the knocking boiler's burnt old heart,
the wheezing heat turned down to stoke the bank.
Gone sweetheart, darling, your lone lumbering
sharp tongue—there's nothing I've forgotten.
Strike one, strike two, the autumn's cauldron hissed
and singed the years' dark pelts until they charred.
Beneath the floor, the antiquated ducts
were partway closed: sloe eyes, they watched
us hunt for candles when the lights blew out.

Midnight in February, Green River, Vermont

When I walked out with you
in the late night hours
I keened for the trees I knew

were there, bone
divining timber
against the pitch-black cold,

and you said, "In summer,
this road is dust all over."
And from deep in the ice-held firs

a bird of dust flew out
and skidded on the frozen cistern
of winter.

Our Listening Audience

A week-old *Times,* face down and open
       to the scores, the jam a coda the tongue
   keeps coming back to, and over the snakeskin base

   of the green metal reading lamp,
the torn shade makes a shadow fin.
   Deep in its own image, the day

flutes inward, a frowzy bit of pillow coming out.
       This is the Saturday New Music Hour.
   In the premonitory, mural dark,

       the briefly coughing program
jars the mind's cartoon. A bent umbrella
   props the window shut,

the eyelet curtain very faintly stirs
       a moth-alarm of wings against the heart.
   Downstairs, the steampipes bang

       and slur the neighbors' caterwaul; a totem mutter
of mother and father, the leopard embrace
   of childhood. What can there be left to hear?

Even now, they go on talking and talking.
       It's four o'clock.
   The brass table is a cymbal for the coffee cup.

       The radio is a German lull, then bleats a broadcast
from the Salzburg Festival. In the ear's small
   blacksmith shop, a TV natters from beyond the wall.

Now

It's spring out, and the acrid
hiss of rain on Madison
heaves in the wake of the buses.

Such a long time we've been sitting here.
The dusty fronds are old green loden coats,
heavy around us, the crushed

clouds of tissue roses are
light-resistant, and a little torn.
Watery, thin, the daylight

is whittled down by the revolving door,
becoming another day
entirely: a scrimshaw of "Later on,

when things get better," that is always in front
and also behind us, junky and bleached,
like the word *now,* that small atom, that pearl.

Wildlife

Head smaller than my fist, pin teeth,
the frightened chipmunk clutching the porch screen
frightens me—quick movement not my own
jarring a rainy, eerie afternoon, in a week
of enforced solitude, as though my heart leapt out.

Time inchoate, meaningless. Two birds,
trapped all night inside the porch, arch and din
against the grid. A day equals
a black year—motor of the blood a drill gone mad.
At dawn we found them, wooed them out.

And then, last night, a mole: visitant friar
at the garbage can. Alone, I stamp my foot,
but, bold in company, one guest terrified, become
benign protector of dim habits, earthly
or unearthly scrounging, in or out.

Failure

Another summer we didn't get through—
the year a dandelion blown to bits,
the clover trampled at the gravel's edge,
the penny-colored leaves glutting the pond,
a file of redwinged blackbirds attentive
in the reeds, their markings military
against the sky, almost navy, filling
with thunderheads. A week full of saluting:
the dam, the mill, the town, the earth, the silver
automobile rusting under the pines,
one door ajar, like a wing. Then the end—
Good-bye house, good-bye pond; the incantations
of children read to in the bath, while night,
angular, conspiring, blackens the glass.

Triptych

ROSE MANNEY ZARIN, 1903–1986

I ST. VINCENT'S

The green pass card is huge, so visitors
can't take it out—

kleptes; the spirit at a loss.

Inner city. At Reception, the guard, chewing gum,
looks up through the bullet-proof divide

and moves his lips. "I.C.U.?"
I see you? Closed breviary, my shut brain
flails, then thumbs—

I see you: the giggly tail
of childhood's favorite game, spider face
smiling through a finger web.

Now flesh stripped down to family bone,
a taut, familiar, czarist streak.

What to see now but how love ends?
Your heartbeat an arrowhead aimed at your heart.

II LAST DAYS

Each hour a mourner, we couldn't leave,
and wakeful, dreaming, each one of us
became another: daughter into mother; father

into daughter; one thralled foot in,
then out of the water. And that first night,
at vigil in the waiting room, on a row

of chairs bolted to the corridor, I lay
awake, unmoving, wedged inside the ribcage
of the chairs' taut arms. Enough

room, if I lay still; my trunk and lungs
a beating, thinking heart. Safe
as when, a child of nearly ten, you afraid

that, visiting, I'd roll and fall,
you put kitchen chairs around my bed. And then
I lay sleepless, afraid of falling.

In the next days,
two decades later, in that apartment
with its long river views, where, it seemed,

my bare feet, swinging, still sung songs
above the wooden floor—childhood, having gone
on there, ended: the black telephone a widow

ringing a black tardy bell, rupturing
my first sleep in fifty hours: *my turn*
to get up and come back down, and, suddenly,

the phone, abstracted, a buzzing vulture,
my legs spindled to shaking castaways, and I,
bowing my head to wash and drink, saw, reflected,

only my greener version of your roan eyes.
Back at the hospital, ten blocks downtown: Fury.
Speech, your darling, had swum off

into a blue-green syringe, and frantic, waving,
you pointed out letters too fast for us to follow
on homemade alphabets that we held up on cards:

a litany of *N*s and *O*s: *No* to sedatives. *No*
to not waking you up to say good-bye (what if . . .)
the same *no* you used for recurring

jokes, in which I was the subject: *Miss No;*
"Cynthia's first word was *no,*" this *no* a fever
dream, a Noh drama; your mouth a hand, primordial,

speaking, a possum clinging to our pulsing arms,
then, palms held together, bored with
dutiful reports on the weather (*important for the patient*

to know life is going on) miming: "What books
have you been reading?" (!)
Answer: alphabet cards—four days

deciphering your hallucination of two twins,
peering at you, downed bird, on your metal bed;
then your remote enormous head in death—

Ma, ma, ma—

That one syllable the first and last.

III   LOSS

No sense in wondering where you are, just
gone; portent of a larger portent.
What's my first loss? A glass chip, dime store
ruby ring. Careless to the last regard,

then final—how to keep count among the dead
and not count in ourselves?

It has no end. The Russian woman made of wooden eggs
hides a tiny ova in her smallest twin,
the Morton's salt girl is a diminishing speck
in endless rainy weather.
"Wear galoshes," said her mother,
over and over again.

Old words: valise, galoshes.
Tea. Ill health.
When I would leave, twilight, sly-footed
cordoning off the city, your imperative,
a lasso, pulled me back:

Call me when you get there

Fabulist of my childhood,
white fingers at my elbow,

now try to answer that.

Bus Ride on Sunday, New York

"I say to her, if you don't need it, what's
the bargain?" *Mirabile dictu,*
the zaftig woman with big mouton sleeves,
fratoozled (her word) up with a corsage,
plays mother on gemutlich TV ads
for VCRs. "I can't go out that I'm
not stopped—if truth be told, they think I'm real."
On Forty-Eighth, the blonde in white gets off;
amazed, the three-card-monte players bow
to Venus, softly risen from their dreams.
"Adorable, the mail I get—*a blessing
from God, to have such sons.*" Then, without pause,
Mouton persuades her friend to get a dog:
"You'll thank me, sweetheart, for the joy it brings."

The Swordfish Tooth

An Erté obelisk, a spire, the solitary
letter *I,* a stopped metronome, cool, wooden,
infinitely beleaguered, bland as an unlit
cigarette. Upright, the swordfish tooth,
a sickbed gift, plays didactic marionette.
Sickness is punishment, says Fever;
like Pinocchio, one's made oneself grotesque
for telling random, half-forgotten lies.
This flu's genesis is Asian—like innocence
of war at home, it fells Americans under forty.

Reviewing the previous week's events,
Christmas is the culprit. Us, childless,
set on by the family's provender
of battery-powered phlegmish angels: maraschino
lights switched on, their sweatshirts
spelled out, infectiously, *Joyeux Noel.*
Two days later found us entombed, punch
drunk on brandy, rose hips, and microbes.
Decades and distance make us orphans,
childhood a loose tooth, tied to a thread.

Simple prayer: If I fall, let it be
on this cottage-cum-house's hand-knotted
turtle and flower Turkish rug. Thus.
After a week of Penguin's recycled
picaresques (pink-cheeked barristers
advising lower-case saints in Dorset)
accompanied by influenza's rites—
chills, headache, complaints, the telephone
unplugged—recovery. Beer all around
to celebrate. The tooth, clinging to grit,

. . .

forlorn, unattached, long as my arm,
washed up by the syzygic tide: Earth, Sun,
and Moon, in what the meteorologists
persist in calling "an unusual line,"
is, if nothing else, a paddle.
And I, a bleary seal in my nightgown,
roused, repentant, still bewitched,
loath to be called an ungrateful child;
the swordfish tooth, non sequitur, a certainty
to cleave the soul back to the spine.

Klex

Klex, an idiomatic shortening of *klecks;* the German word for "inkblot" was the nickname of Hermann Rorschach, the Swiss psychiatrist and inventor of the Rorschach test, during his school days in Zurich.

One reads whatever comes to hand. At the beach,
A Guide to Seashells, or *Fifty Ways To Make
Good Chowder;* lacking that, the proverbial
joke, the label on the aspirin bottle.
Cambridge, after Cape Cod's austerities—gravel,
salt, books stinking of damp—is a prelapsarian
testament, the molten tropes of student lamps
august, cerebral, a projected, planar, Eden.
Also the rest: numbers, begating, exodus.
Here overnight to catch a morning plane, a lazy
serendipitous review, at bedtime, of Cotton Mather
—*Bonifacius*—wards off Cambridge's preemptive
strike, by Zion's silver rattle, teethed on:
the fear that one remembers nothing.

New England's tightwad glamour is deep snow.
After Boston traffic's seventh circle, where,
concommitant, we drive in circles, one's grateful
to be aloft at all. A mile below, the coastline,
like Klex, solemn, Swiss, resolves at that distance
to his test—guilt at lax domesticity
extending (as Mr. Miller writes of Shepard's
Covenant) unbroken, from Abraham to Boston,
the familiar turned uncanny, admonitory:
a pond; an iron skillet left to soak
and rust, and, black swan beneath a covered
bridge; a zipper gagging on a safety pin;
the black sentence of a nursery hymn played
idly, obsessively, on the piano's minor keys.

And no wonder, when simply to pull
one's sweater off—arms crossed, lifted—
is to be thrown back, marooned in a dark
mime of dead man's float. Even one's own name,
spelled carefully into the telephone becomes
a cipher, doodled fifty times, elaborately,
while stuck on hold; the blotter a signed
transcript of confessional, the rushing
letters turned to arrows, lunar, Greek—
For Rorschach, in the *Kantonschulle,* "Klex,"
the nickname a leaky palindrome, moored
between the present and the future tense;
blue inkblots creased to handprint butterflies
the pupa of the *Psychodiagnostik.*

One misreads according to one's lights,
sputtered tallow differing from murky green
in the old Reading Room; against the snow,
the Saints a negative of burning candlewicks;
and under the eyelid of an afternoon
(Boston to Newark, then a taxi) a glance
reads *dangerous* for "diligence," *potato*
for "platelet," adding, latterly, the melody
of a sighing *Oh* in place of the embattled tsk
of consonants; each day a sermon read aloud
illuminated by the heart's topaz; history's
inkwell held aloft and spilled, drop by
drop, on actual paper, folded, revelatory—
balking, like Mather, at no reproof.

Pears Soap

FOR ROBERT FITZGERALD

Transparence a virtue, as in prose or water,
though not lies; like good news from a far country,
the Pears soap's rider of ingredients—thyme, cedar,
glycerine—comes affiched with a baroque postage
stamp, a filigree signet, familiar as a cigar band:
by appointment to Her Majesty the Queen, since

seventeen-eighty-nine; the year (one looks it up)
Eclipse, the famous racehorse, died; Blake published *Songs
of Innocence,* and, boarded with its Latin cousins,
fuchsia and hortensia, the chrysanthemum
was introduced from the Orient, into England.
Also the year King George, mad, retrieved his senses.

Through the yellow bathroom's frosted glass, the urban
morning is a dun frieze, a grisaille, and the gold
soap a chrysalis; a stained glass lozenge, a pane
from the neverending Thragelia: harvest
of soot, getting over it, sorrow a fly
in amber—Chryseis, back in Rome, after Apollo's

pestilence; Blake's boy in his chrome chrysanthemum,
glad after experience, and the soap, slipped from
my wrinkling hand, a bronze-winged partridge, squatting on
the porcelain—partridge a Midlands alias
of Roman umber—its name washing off but its
clear self still left, reversal of the usual death.

from

FIRE LYRIC

(1993)

The Box Turtle

Long-lived, repository of memory; secretive,
not outgoing; the turtle, knowledgeable of
inner regions—*terra anima,* terraqueous—
    gives its heart once, and not far.

Slow moving under the salmon snapdragons,
the cucumber's umbrella leaves, the
raspberries' jewelled Palace of the Doges,
    this summer's box turtle sunning on

the flagstones is last summer's same Trojan,
its head a thumb on the ground's warm
throb, testing for action, for salinity,
    for how our incursions should deflect his

or her dependable intentions. It is
only we who think of change. Beauty's gaze
has no new eye; its inverse is
    not ugliness but shame: the turtle

unnamed but for description recoils only
as encroached on. Its belly markings shadowy,
once exactly handprint-sized; the garden prince,
    at first love, aged five—one hand

good enough for counting, one turtle
consort—who now despairs of finding ever again
the very same calciferous hide, calling
    its name, "Turtle," in the compost.

Not a stir. Tristan, last year's boy,
scans from inside this year's whistling and

contracting boreal signs, and the turtle
    wished on as a circumscriber is

in hiding. We know the boy is the same,
and not the same. We know the zenith sun
has its own sequestered dark spots; that
    the world is tigerish, like a debutante

looking both to stay and quick be gone—hesitant,
empyrean; that the turtle's stately box step
cuts in, and keeps one dancing, *terra*
    a terra, in the same bright circle.

Far Abbotsbury

All in a line in Cow Harbor, out past
the geranium dry dock, just wet down, the goslings—no
      taller than the *infanta* irises—that swim

in the ear shape of the pitcher bay are not
the swans in Abbotsbury, where "the medieval
      lingers, and the past strikes the eye," where

from the pebbly stretch of beach one can see
seven white spires, each one a swan's neck. Here,
         in our harbor, you can count three

striped umbrellas—white and yellow—five geraniums, the
Travel section, and these geese, begging bread
      in the parenthesis formed by the gravel

and the inlet. Due east, down Hardy's rainy oak
the days are plunder, beneath its boughs the goosegirl
      counts her flocks—she is never

without them—but here they are, transmogrified.
Who is to say that the worn goosegirl is not a princess,
      and these fowl not peering swans, or that

the masts of the catboats are not steeples, for
through them the wind sings? Too small
         to make much noise, the young are nonetheless

protected, their Victorian parents press them to
the bread, and beyond the Atlantic's great
         sucking waves, at the eight-mile swannery

. . .

in Abbotsbury, the swanherd, for a small sum,
will give commentary: The birds should not be called
    if there is no sustenance, for they are

vicious; we are unprotected from their beauty; their song
holds captives and is captivating, to swans we stand
    for nothing. Incidental, in this watery

sunshine, to say the same for goslings.

The Cormorants

The cormorants are braying and neighing, clogging
   the harbor, the scarp, and the little beach

where the boat is, like a raft of mismatched brown
   boots fitting no one, their worn tops listing

to port and to starboard, a hazard in the mud room.
      Why have they come here? Everyone agrees it's

unusual to see even two or three a summer. Other,
   pleasanter birds have vanished, and we have

these in return, bellowing, dropping what must be
         their very innards on the skiffs, feeding

their offspring—who look like small, feckless
         thunderclouds painted by a dabbler who

wants to get everything in—by regurgitation.
         Like *piñatas,* each boat has a coat of their

Plaster-of-Paris. Each bird chokes and muzzles.
      Their smoke-ring routes take them

nowhere and on returning they never have
      enough perches. They push each other aside

in a clumsy game of musical chairs, or like
      tourists hastily assembled in the heat who

all want to sit next to the driver. But there is
         no driver. Whoever is first gets a seat

on the foremast. In China, cormorants wearing
      neck-rings were tamed and made to catch fish,

but no one here has the least idea if they still
      do this. Now, at low tide, their cries

make great ellipses, binding the trawls, the dock,
      the whole quiet town, from which Atwood's

Shoes, the candy store, the white horse we
      used to see, and even the Post Office,

has disappeared. Everyone is at the beach.
      By winter, the cormorants will be gone too,

taking with them whatever it was they liked
      and saw—a shoelace, a pocket knife, your

Blackfoot drawing pencil, the hours spent
      cleaning up after them, scraps of torn news.

The Pamet Puma

Puma, cougar, mountain lion, loup—
    this is what I am afraid of, Ocarina,
small singing goose in the break-ax
wood, that you will be gone, and in
              your place

fur moving, indistinguishable from sand.
    The Pamet River rides to salt, the dunes
are hills of thunder, the sky
doesn't fall because you don't think
             of it,

but those vines you nest in
    are the tops of buried trees, two eyes
shine like spearmint in the witch
grass, and even your voice neither
            persuades

nor dissuades him. He will not come out.
    The syrinx doesn't call him. He knows
the place where the lamb lies down.
You who keep yourself to yourself,
            who have

your own face on, who know that loup
    means mask, loup-garou a werewolf,
and catamount is any wild cat, bay-lynx
is the end of trying to put
            a name

to him, *Rufus* of the Atlantic,
    the bobcat. Apples in a moon-pail

of water, outline of dry bones
on a doorsill, spine of a dogbane
                    leaf

that prevents speech, a fish jaw
        that won't go down: all say, "bob
means to strike." But the puma
isn't curious. His prints are
                    carbon,

his coat is fire, and I, who dress
        my fear to talk it down, want to shelter
you in the barberries—you, who don't
court trouble, who won't search for the
                    needle

in the haystack, who beating two
        flat stones together merely laugh:
puma, catamount, panther, bobcat,
the aim of the boomerang is not to
                    come back.

Fire Lyric

Three flames
on a branched
candlestick.

One is Wick,
another
Tender,

the third
Pitch. Pitch
is gone.

Wick and
Tender are
two steamship

vents. Then
each in Alice
blue, two

can-can
dancers.
Then ghosts.

Tender's
out. Gold but
with a heart

of ash, Wick's
an owl on
a matchstick.

. . .

Feathers
singe in that
harsh hiss.

Topaz flares
two times
in the pier

glass—third eye
to find her
sisters there.

The Ant Hill

Sand pyramid, size of a child, each September
    it was moved thirty feet back from the veranda's
        longest shadow, which stopped in its daily

violet slope near the withering yew. Moved gently,
    with a wide flat shovel. From the kitchen,
        the wrecked hill was a slag heap, its mussel

color germinating in rain to brown, to velvet, to mica
    so that after a time a reflection shone from it
        and scattered, and each June, Mother said aloud

that it seemed the house moved closer to the hill,
    even though the hill was long moved back.
        For the little girls who watched, who heard,

each tremble-leg was a signal in their own patois,
    a wave good-bye, the whole a black bead curtain
        like the one at Mrs. Hennessey's, where sometimes,

of an afternoon, they were left—her doorway with its
    there, not there, its speechless partings, the
        dark italic hedge too small to read. A decade

of exile: of school, of being sent to bed, of being
    told to put the book down, as every year the ants
        were wrenched from their own tenacious fondness

for the veranda pilings, for the black blossoms of old tires
    that clung to them like clematis until—a moving
        picture of transit—the ants crossed over again

. . .

for their mysterious attendance on the flagstones,
    the hill again grown pointed, night-colored, earth
        turned to mirror-water, a satellite by

the fence post that was flattened, excavated, removed.
    And then the white house was a flipped coin,
        by and by deserted, its face showing not

the sun but the moon, and the girls who drew with a stick
    under the yew and learned their letters now
        stood under its cracked limbs to bicker, to

divide the world between them, to say what Mother
    said, to speak too subtly, about the ant hill now
        taller than the pilings, the veranda

turned violet as its shadow.

The Opossum's Dream

FOR JACK

Opossum
I hang from
the limb

of sleep,
hip to thigh
and thigh to

knee, and in
my dream
become a

leaf, tail to
sprout and skin
to green, a

leaf holding
fast to the
big tree, twig

to turn and
breeze to free.
Then stem to

breath and bud
to sleek, I
feel myself

in my night
dream, rib to
fin and gill

. . .

to breathe,
become a
trout, swimming

downstream fast
to the wide
sea, scale to

flash, grass to
weed, and at
the river's mouth

I feel, fresh
to salt and
mute to bark,

the trout I
am become
a seal, gliding

slow and warm,
deep beneath,
who bobs her

head up to
inquire, *Is
it morning?*

—But no,
the stars
are fired—

and diving
down becomes
a whale, dark

. . .

and huge, a world
entire—
seas and farms,

towns and fields,
breathing deep
until I feel

the sleep I'm
sleeping is
a bear's, who

curling in
his shambled
dream, fur

to wing and
tooth to beak,
dreams himself

small and
is a bird—
a bird who

stirs and sings:
I am a boy
asleep

in the green
tree's arms . . .
Opossum

I hang from
the limb
of sleep.

The Vestal Birches

Wort and sphagnum rib the lichen frieze
    where messenger on a Greek urn, an orange
    newt balks steadily. You down
        below in your new house! A world
        glides to white, as autumn mists

turn the mountain threnodial, its
    flaring notes the birches' stopped cold flame! Out past
    your neighbor's gravel pit, we
        sorted through furred junk on someone
        else's porch: shoe trees, a child's

blue chair, a hurricane lamp. A dun
    fly-swatter was a magic wand: aloft, a
    beggar's arm in creeping dark.
        What statesman's house did we two stop
        at once, freighted with sorrow

on our way North? Pitched tents of gnarled roses
    filled the shuddery parlor, their wizened
    blossoms kitten faces. They
        mewed behind us as we drove, then
        turned to birds. Gold in the black

birches flew. Now your letters whistle
    on their own, blown glass blooms above their
    finished stems. "It was Grant's
        lodge," you write, "where he spent his last
        months scrawling down his life. And

here's another detail of that day—
    the house is now inside a jail." My dear, my

mind had left that embrace out
    and gentle kept that summer's day
    a dreaming if not tearful

eye. In its attic gaze I had us
    walk there still. I had two deer—it doesn't
matter now—intelligent,
      who broke the woods and turned. Any
      place is where we could not live.

The Skunk on Commercial Street

(NEW YEAR'S DAY, PROVINCETOWN)

Black and white, the skunk, low-
    slung, stumped slowly down
    the street's white line
        as if road

and animal were one
    design. We pointed,
    stared. Chaplin, who
        worried he

would not be remembered,
    was, that dawn the skunk
    tracked Snow Street's slant
        downward to

the beach, a Portobello
    with its shelf of wrecks:
    shells; a Christmas
        tree, black as

a big mascara wand;
    a battered license
    plate, as if bored,
        a car had

sprouted working fins or
    wings. Stalled, creatural,
    sleepy in our
        too-bright clothes,

we sniffed the air. Just salt
and wet, tar with its
winter stink of
marigolds.

Then we saw her pause and
seem to preen. Firm in
voluminous
solitude,

wed to her operatic
cloak and her perfume,
she shrugged as if
to say, *What's*

black or white to me?
Limber before day's
hard gold gong, the
skunk trod west

across the macadam
until she might have
been a white cap
in the bay

waving to the town's white
pantomime, blackness
behind her as
New Year broke.

The Hare

Singular—Durer's—crouched, alert, stock-
still; the hare caught now in April's
    bevelled glass is the past, in perpetuity;

windy gloom, rain-soaked papers flying—daylight
twitching in and out of clouds—I saw
    you, book-laden, hurrying round

the passage to the Music Room, where,
bound in Bach cantatas for an afternoon, you
    would be, you said, beset by love. Love

was a horn player, I remember, who
strolled off to fortune and bad temper: Vienna,
    Hamburg, Beacon Hill. Then the hourglass's

southern hemisphere: doldrums, and the Key
West pier. Cheeks flame, chin squared, playing
    beneath a battered Durer print; you

barely bellowed out your rage when spurned
—his mistake—and survived instead on greens
    and horrible cream cakes. Audile,

benign, sole icon of the practice room, to me,
the hare *was* yours. But now, glossy in some
    gallery spread, it's been rent, from you,

as you are gone from who you were once
then, all concentration on crescendo, your viola
    drowning out bird warble in

those fledgling dusks, the gaze above
your head arrested, as I was too—*d'amore*
   stung become Orion's horn.

Learning German

I

Barbed letters a bramble or thicket
I couldn't leave be, a language
to make mistakes in. Later you
 read to me in your beautiful voice,

Od und leer das Meer, then *Jeder
Engel ist schrecklich.* Leader in
staged childhood wars, your passion-
 note rang on the grammar

school triangle. Sounding, it
ruined the bravura of Mozart's G
Minor by chanting, to the bleat
 of the quartet's

first bars, *An-swer the telephone.*
At eight, our age is what we
are. Spread-limbed on the polar bear,
 we mapped our bluish arteries

with your mother's carmine lip-
stick, Splendor Red. Next
to the phonograph in your house,
 where I'd come to play,

a book of photographs, gray bodies
piled to make an astonishing
wall. Eyes, a foot, a hand hung
 out, breaking the smooth

fish surface.

II

A wall as high as fear could go. And on
the wall that history built, an entire
self built out of doubt, and that doubter
told to believe, someone will read
a message hidden in a wall of tears:

      here are the songs sung in the bath
the murmur at the window at the baby
the song before sleep bows its head
the mutter at the door at bad news
the greeting on good luck, the whisper
of awe, the edge of silence, a bare foot
that traces out a groove the racing
      water fills, so that *lied*
sounds more dear than any troubadour's romance
the song of gladness in an orange beak
and in that tenderness a shriek.

III

A swish of wings on the triangle's silver
    tangent, that same silver in a long hair
        that stole into Great-Grandmother's

black braid. She pulled it tight, then out:
    before her hair turned white she'd spun
        the shimmying line that kept *us*—

ephemeral, unreal, gossiping then of nothing,
    odd spoons in the spheres—out of
        the gas. And managed, even, that time

. . .

might still be bounded by the compass's snail
    track, so that I, a child, could watch
       her daughter with her shining hand

transplant ivy from a coffee can into a fishbowl
    garden that shed tears to breathe.
       Miniature as a man made out of glass

I plant my foot here in the paved city street,
    made Venetian by its grays and greens, gently
       as any of the unlocated, the

unpossessed, who knew, before the news
    of plate tectonics, that the world had split,
       who, brought up by coincidence know

as well as if their palm lines spelled it out in
    shorthand dutifully taken down from
       the seemingly voiceless, the only ones

who speak: any hour holds your death. There is
    no moment between now and what comes next.
       One plucks at strings to breathe

a measured line: why would I, between one November
    and a New Year, take up a German grammar,
       dictionary and text, and try for weeks

to learn to read and speak a language that if
    I ever used I wouldn't need in the semblance
       the old books I chose supplied?

Speaking only to myself I learned to say, that
    warm winter, that my cow had died, my dress
        was torn, that it was cold, that I had

forgotten my papers, that *traumen* meant "to dream."

IV

Don't swim at the college pool
    where a peculiar lather
of the light turns the shower-
    heads to Chinese characters

that spell out as clear as any
    Gothic letters ever could:
Death, Delusion, Danger, Fool.
    And when two German students

happy on exchange, enter
    chattering into the hot
wood sauna where you blankly
    lie, half sleeping, naked,

you simply rise, go. Think
    no further than, "It's
time." Don't wish, *Liebchen,*
    for a baby with blue eyes.

V

Through the bucket's hole the gathered water
    flows like giant tears. Unstoppable,

. . .

the bucket, the mangled giant, and those grim
    tears, unmendable as a propensity

to fear, a quartet forever halted by
    a few words too often spoken, to a haltered

horse, his nightmare painted on his blinders,
    who wanders his own switchback route,

erloschen. Answer it then, the telephone
    that rings, stops, and rings. Wires

cross like crows over the ribs of ocean
    and when you answer someone breathes out

melodies, as if the swimming clouds were
    speaking fish, a carmine sunset

that will not ebb until it is forgiven
    for also having feelings . . . And we can

only answer the voice from the primer we
    were given, the one that names each part

aloud: Here is a nose, here is your chin,
    that says, tasting the earth in its mouth:

The dress is in the meadow having a dream.

Thee and Lew Freeman

Up and down the road the old car went.
　　This is a story that my aunt
told me, decades later on a warm
　　June afternoon. I can't say why
it stuck with me so long, but some things
　　worry me that way, and Thee and
Lew Freeman—no one knew anybody with
　　those names. I knew the landscape
of the story though, so I heard it like
　　an illustrated book—the dock,
the Pamet River, the lock, the places
　　where the pine trees shook.
We always talk of houses, my aunt and
　　I—I haven't got one and she
thinks a house is a fine thing for someone
　　to have. I have to say that
I do too. But that day she told me about
　　her friend, who had a son, who
at seven had imaginary friends. They
　　weren't children, which was
strange, and as I've said, Thee and
　　Lew Freeman were their names.
But once he told their names he wouldn't
　　let it be, but said he had to
visit Thee. Lew didn't come in for quite
　　so much talk. Once in a while
he'd be around the place, up on a
　　ladder. Or he'd answer the door.
Or so the boy described it to his
　　mother, who, good-naturedly,
agreed to drive him here and there until
　　he found the house that Thee

and Lew belonged to. It was in
    the neighborhood, he said, just
a little out of town, and for a day
    or two she drove and followed
his directions, turning off the road
    at one or another clump of trees.

On the third day, my aunt told me,
    her friend said something about
it being silly, wasn't it, driving
    in circles to look for Thee.
It was then the boy seemed to make
    his mind up, and had his mother
turn and turn along the dusty road
    until they came to a white house
on a hill. That was the house, he said,
    where Thee and Lew lived. They
had two cats, a dog named Moose.
    They ate pork and beans. My
aunt clearly remembered this, and said
    that her friend asked her boy
if he would like to go on up and say
    hello, but he refused. Oddly, after
that, he never spoke of them. It
    was as if they'd never been.
And soon our conversation changed, to
    whether casement windows are
prettier than plate, and if I thought
    the porch door needed paint.

But now, for no reason I can say, I think
    of Thee and Lew as mine. They
have those two cats still, which is
    impossible, though before I got
there they gave the dog away—he bit.

. . .

The cats are Hector and Geronimo.
Winter or summer, the ball goes to and fro.
    But I like to see them of
an evening, Thee and Lew. They like to
    talk, you see, and think aloud.
And sometimes Thee will sing to me
    of places where I've never
been, but given half a chance I'd go.

Old Landscape, Umbria

The animosity of the inanimate doesn't
        accommodate. See where the stone shimmers,
            where wind has washed the face of the Rocca

to the color of poppies at dusk, to
        ash. Down too, the steady ilex grows and crowns
            the hill, scrambling for purchase as the screech

owl does, who returns no matter what: he wants to own
        the place where he lives. Loosestrife clogs the road,
            asphalt crumples—one understands as a child of

nature does the impulse to paint over all the frescos
        in San Francesco though civility applauds the counter-
            impulse that lets the marble dog go on

eating grapes on the facade of San Pietro at Spoleto,
        a church itself built on the wrack of a Roman
            cemetery, where today, in the dust, a woman complains

she has been left alone. Her own white dog
        has run off all the way down here from Monteluco.
            Finally, here is her son to take her home in a

car. Tender, he holds the captured Alsatian in his arms.
        The dog wears a red collar and a pleased look,
            he is no kin to the tiny dog who writhes under the weight

of his marble garland, a motif echoed in a second
        church, three kilometers up, where once again, after
            a gap of only ten or eleven centuries, marriages

. . .

are occurring. Only for this moment are we not
        figures in stone. Only now as, accommodating, we
                hand over coins to the curate for the San Giuliano

restoration fund, a man whose deftness is surprising
        in one so old, so deaf, who shows us the view down to
                San Pietro, where the dog is still gone mad, do the leaves

even answer our breath, do twigs move on the landscape's
        latticed crown—the distant hill flecked with
                explosions of poppies where now perhaps from sheer

incredulity the boy who tends the sheep after school
        thinks of the lady who was afraid of the dogs, who
                couldn't speak, who waved from the window,

who vanished. Like and unlike the Etruscans, who near here
        barely left a language, but who mapped the sacred wood
                so well they could not help but enter it.

White Violets in South Hadley

So many of them wicking the lawns—
a hundred handkerchiefs dropped
by the daughters of the Pleiades
to mask their seven-square fears.

Their gold is the hive's dry dust—
their petals a thousand small white knuckles . . .

On Faculty Lane, the whiteness
of the dogwood bleaches their white
bank to almost nothing, ghosts of
ghosts, damp violet coals burnt out,

as if a bruise that seemed to leave no mark
had left the image of its pressure here.

Ruby at Auction

FOR VICKIE KARP

The question is, whose was it? Darker than
the finest quality Thai ruby; mined, most
likely, a century ago in Burma, this stone
—clear sight's happy obstacle—is not,

however, typically Burmese. Deeper than
the hue of pigeon's blood, oxblood bindings
on *The Collected Works of—*, or Pomerol:
the setting is original. Mr. Block,

the auctioneer, is sure of this but shaky
on its provenance. Might as well say blood
will tell—he fans the cards, then picks.
The Mandalay? Seen last at Christie's, London,

eighteen-ninety-six? Decades gone, the stone
in its snowstorm of diamonds pocketed,
secreted, kept through hoop-rolling, Flanders'
poppy, the blitz. By now the jewel is pour

and tor, an owl's heart, a rosehip, gemology's
Gioconda, Mars in a tilt sky remote from
the mild blue of Mandalay: the largest ruby
ever auctioned, outlasting love or sentiment.

Of Lincoln

Of Lincoln we know next to
nothing, when we consider we have not
heard his voice. No turning black wheel
    holds it, no radio wave nor

electronic bird's wing carries
it. We know his oceanic beard, his
unrelieved profile, imagine
    a certain habit of tenderness

born from disarming passion, but
he is not fixed in the cocked heart
which is our listening ear. Gunshots
    blossom from tin moments, moss

grows on the cave painting
hieroglyph, fluency begrimed is hatred's
lullaby, but the last trumpet note
    blown in the sanctuary

is held by the hand that cups
it. "The mind is the standard of
the man," said Dr. King, and we can
    hear him saying it. The

standard demands that we reckon
the equation of feathers and bricks
and find both tons the same
    though we know otherwise,

the blueprint of our monuments
calls for wooden wheels rocketing
over paving stones but this year,
    pausing, we can learn

from the contents of a mouse-
chewed shoebox found in a Springfield
attic that Lincoln asked, defending, "Did
    Greek hit him first?" and

that he himself staged a fight
for the benefit of the jury. If
sound is blazoned particles and matter
    is moving, then this

paper wrested from the Shades
vibrates with a voice loud with field
smoke and pine song from its sojourn at
    the stove pipe. And we again

imagine what it might have said to
us, and see the body like a feather
falling, and hear again the sound a light
    thing owns when it hits.

The Mechanical Arm

How can we begin to bear what we don't have?
    And then to feel, in empty space,
an arc of movement, far removed? Still, its
    barely stenciled hand points to a Palace

of Lost Things, where atomic glitter once erased
    is reconstructed better than before
a moment got the best of what we had, replacing
    it with absence. The century fills. Signac

wrote that though Seurat's father had lost an arm,
    he used it nonetheless to carve a brace
of partridges, a roast, and two fowl. His pace
    bordered on showmanship. Gleaming, the steel

and pulley arm sliced and cut above the ironed lace
    as deft as, in a life removed, his own son's
swift untethered hand would disassemble what it saw,
    then paint light's stilt-walk back in place.

Song

FOR ROSE

My heart, my dove, my snail, my sail, my
   milktooth, shadow, sparrow, fingernail,
      flower-cat and blossom-hedge, mandrake

root now put to bed, moonshell, sea-swell,
   manatee, emerald shining back at me,
      nutmeg, quince, tea leaf and bone, zither,

cymbal, xylophone; paper, scissors, then
   there's stone—Who doesn't come through the door
      to get home?

from

THE WATERCOURSE

(2002)

Spode Plate

TO HARRY AND KATHLEEN FORD

A branch sprouting from its crook a chrysanthemum,
and below, new leaves, a grass snake, a pale line

in the glaze that between us, we can call a river.
Stars, smatterings of the old crowd—Andromeda, Orion,

the bear cub, and now, far off, you. How in heaven
did the plate get so dirty? I rinse it with soap

and water, I scrub like a child taught to have faith
in washing, then furiously, my back a question

mark, my hunch the crouch of a crone with an ear
to the ground, a doubter, but a cloud remains

over the flaring sun and the coiled serpent, smudging
the wry plain of stars. I didn't know this could happen.

I thought if you scrubbed, the stain would dissolve in
the water used to douse it, and the scene—the burning

tree with its too-heavy bright bloom, the black stars
on the charred hill, the ragged maiden—would again

be a place that had heard nothing, and seen less,
a landscape of mild temperance, the smooth porcelain

alive with the sheen of reflected moonlight, where Orion
could shoot the bear along the river, and miss, and miss.

Harriet

Why did I say what I did to Harriet?
She was my age: nine, I don't think ten—
a kind of taunting I'd not do again.
Not to Harriet, who for me still
limps up the hill, jacket torn, stained skirt rent.
Harriet who wasn't beautiful yet.
Monster is what the mirror said to me—
I opened my mouth and Harriet fled.
Now those words are breath, there's no sound
but the hissing wind in the wild trees,
and Harriet falling, as she didn't then.

Bruise

Black bruise an inch
below my knee; white bone, my
    kneecap wrenched askew;

        knee a blind eye, bruise
a shiner, the pair of them two
    goggle-eyes, bridged by

        a shiny, half-moon scar.
A battered aviatrix? She
    flies above a dream island.

        At three, I fell from
a knee-high curb. *Mind yourself,*
    I hear the voices say,

        when decades later,
in the bath, my knee, drowned
    face, knucklehead, rises

        above the water table,
volcano with its violet flame.
    Bedpost? Doorjamb?

        The hours last week
turned to glass? And if asked
    to swear to it, say

        what's to blame?
The mind trolls, reels back,
    and begins, and begins

. . .

again to prove how if
I'd only done that one thing—
but there are so many.

The Astronomical Hen

Like hearts marked out but not yet colored in,
Each of her feathers has a black edge,
as if an India-ink mantilla stretched

from uncleaved neck to her fantail. The pen,
homemade, spilled some darkness now and then.
She doesn't lack for suitors. Poor rooster,

who pours his own loud heart out to her,
surely his begging does no more than force
her to peck out a crooked tattoo in the dirt

of the pen. Is she stumped, sad, anorexic?
It's perfectly clear she doesn't lay eggs.
Can it be she's simply in love with herself?

Her eye obsidian, eye of the world,
at night she watches the stars drop from shelf
to shelf, to minor études she unfurls

in her head. By day she hunts and re-pecks
the pinprick holes of her intricate sketch.
If she's done by dusk the first stars can rise.

Mrs. Donleavey

"There's Mrs. Donleavey," someone said,
and pointed to where she stood in her cloud
of nightgown, twenty yards up from where

five of us waited for the school bus to stop.
Her flood of gold hair was stained with damp.
Rosebuds grew from the gauze and marl

of her body. She hummed, and the long
braid of sound came down to us, a blind snake
in the garden, and though I held back I wanted

to leap and catch it, to grapple, to hoist
myself up into what I even then knew would be
the lap of grief. It was a cool morning

in early spring. Dew polished the dragon
leaves of the laurel, the blue hydrangea,
the boxwood whose dense green scales sprang

back at my touch, from my hand that blocked
her from view when the bus pulled away
with me at the window, and my palm left a smudge

that within days came to mark like a plume
of smoke her complete disappearance
from our street—or so I thought I'd heard,

under a rush of water and the radio—into
a past I believed was hers only, and that
seemed to me then sheer, inconsolable, new.

On Reading a Collected Letters

FOR WILLIAM MAXWELL

The rationing, the slugs on the lawn, the spirit
    lamp casting up the mute face of
    the charwoman's dead child, the elephantine
        car that made it through another

winter, the hoarfrost dotting the lawn. An utter
    frenzy of communication, of agendas
    surprisingly fulfilled in the glossy umber
        evenings with—downstairs—the wireless

going, each typed letter (for later, she typed
    them) a stitch in the seam every so
    often righted by an exclamation, a scrawled
        postscript, glad at the prospect of

a real visit. Tea and scones. The peanut butter
    it was impossible to get in Hampstead
    arriving in the post, kites the Folies-
        Bergère colors of tulips

on Tuesday over the downs, then rain—a torrent—
    on Whitsun which finished off
    the raspberries; all this welter
        of stamps and paper a dumb show

of feeling, the wood, now that it's so hard
    to get warm, chopped by the extraordinary
    Mr. Pillager, who is so faithful about
        lending a hand, whose wife

has a gold sewing scissor shaped like a crane
    with a garnet eye, which was given

to her by her "previous employment."
    But this hand lent, given

to correspondence, to writing salutations
    and envoys, the light blue envelope
    the same color as the sky above
        Euston Station where she always

bought a same-day return, the torn half
    marking the lost chapter of the story
    which is silent in these pages,
        measured out now in centimeters,

sausages and jam, a deliberate feigned ignorance
    that some things are being done
    for the last time, but for a few italicizations—
        a snow goose, an illness—until

she herself is like a signature gone quill-thin
    but nevertheless possible to make out
    under a strong reading lamp, kept on
        past midnight by the thought

of her having just now gone out, as if
    for stamps and paper, carried—a deliverance
    through those light-as-air
        just wide enough doors.

Eclogue

TO AMY CLAMPITT

"Our neighbor, a retired engineer, comes to clip
our hedge, the cardinals come in pairs, but sometimes
singly—their red is black against the lap of green."
Lenox in August, the high blood brick front of the library
peeling white. *I wish, I wish*—the helicopter seeds
of the plane trees spin but do not touch your door.
I wish—onstage the dollmaker's daughter springs
to life, the Nutcracker Prince rides the swan boat.
You do not stir. Tableau vivant, you sail out
on your white bed. We went from you to Wharton's
Mount. Only Rose, in her third summer, braved
the No Admittance sign. "Hullo," she said, "Papa's
calling me." Her exit is her entrance, the words
summer afternoon skittering like hoops down the hill.

Envoy

Every premonition has its points. The *Coronation*
Mass turns on by itself; one candle sheds
more light than another; black thread unspools
and winds around a leg. Primroses for the dead:
when the Mayor called to offer you a place
on San Michele, the opera house went up in flames.
Fenice? True, every phoenix needs its ash, but
nothing, Joseph, is more surprising then surprise.
Radiant cruciform, lit harbor of cherry trees, sky
marbled with dusk, the children a flock of anemones,
of finches—headless as Actaeon I return
to the garden and see you, heart in my mouth,
in your ninth life, searching the flagstones,
calling *Kitty, Kitty,* from the top of the stairs.

The Zoo in Winter

FOR BEATRICE

In the one warm day between two spheres
of cold—a day just warm enough to breathe—
we took the bus to see the zoo in winter.
Every branch and leaf was furred with ice.
At the sea lion pond, spray had sifted
sugar swirls around the rim (we couldn't see
through the glass for the white), but once
or twice a face peered out, a glimpse through lace
at a window. In the penguin house
the penguins never for a moment stopped diving
and drying their piano-key wings in the cold.
A man cleaned the rocks with a huge mop—
an octopus that sat on top of its pole
like a fright wig. No one else came in.
Outside we were joined by a whole family
of children, each one a half-step smaller
than another, like notes on a xylophone.
There was a baby in a stroller. The polar
bear cub played with a ball and a block,
just like a real baby. We worried when
he came too close to the edge, batting his ball
with his sharp claws, and using the block
as a stepping-stone. Most of the water
was frozen over. His mother was sleeping.
The children, all six of them, wanted only
to climb the slippery, icy steps, to hide
themselves from the bear. *Watch out,*
    their mother said, *Hold on.*

The bear went on playing with his ball.
In a tank beside him, two harbor seals
swam swift as muskrats back and forth

. . .

under the green water, which by splashing
continuously over the barricade had left
a tiny seal of ice on the pavement
—snout, tail, shiny tilted head—as if
even it couldn't resist making something
    out of the cold.

Santuario de Chimayó

(NEW MEXICO)

We thought the church would be bigger
but really it was no bigger than a one-room
  schoolhouse. Inside there were pictures
    everywhere, painted on the walls,
      the ceiling, even on the awkward
        homely pews which had been brought
          at great expense from

Española. The walls seemed to
breathe, or maybe it was that we were all of us
  inside a body, breathing in
    together. It was just as I'd
      imagined it might be to enter
      a retablo. I have one
        now on my bookshelf,

a hat seller, hawking twenty
black-and-fawn hats, and often I go over them
  very closely, to discover
    the telling detail—a tipped brim,
      a band—to determine which I should
      choose for the day. But really
        the hats are attached

      to the rafters, and would just fit
my index finger. In niches along the walls
  at Chimayó, the saints, even
    those whose faces are ill drawn or
      whose postures are lackadaisical,
      are clearly scholars, each one
        kept long after to

. . .

learn the complicated verses
of suffering which at any moment they will
be called upon to repeat. Of
the assembled, San Rafael
is the most attentive, his black eyes
astonished. Is he simply
grateful for being

able to see? His gauchos are
red as a turkey wattle, and one of his wings
is dented—I like to think it
was knocked awry in his travels—
but in any case his wings, drawn here,
are more like the staunch colorful flags
or starched banners of

a country whose stamps show views
of mangoes and palms, where every breath of air is
remarked, where the fragile peeling
houses kneel on their legs like
spoonbills and are flooded each spring by
the exhaled water of flush
estuaries. But

there's only the one river in
the place he comes from. The fish he holds is just now
about to turn into a loaf
of bread, bread that by its nature
must be continually replaced
in the mouths of the hungry.
In Chimayó, at

. . .

the spot that became sanctified,
Don Bernando Abyeta, moved by a vision
touched his tongue to the earth and was
cured of what books only describe
as "his illness." Behind the nave, in
a room where had there been one
a younger priest might

have read and slept, the place he marked
in the floor never deepens, though for almost two
hundred years the dirt has been licked
and tasted. In the face of such clear
evidence hardly anyone
who comes resists leaving word,
for taped or pinned up

on the walls like white butterflies
are handwritten requests for help. Near the door
hang discarded crutches: big, picked-
clean wing bones, strong as anyone,
man or angel, might wish for. Why is it
impossible for me to
leave the notes unread,

as if here and only here was
an answer? We left the chapel without tasting
the dirt or writing a message.
Outside our breath froze in the thin
cold air of the sharp mountains, which
had three times seen the cross dug
up at Chimayó,

. . .

        and three times seen it return there
of its own accord. It was as in a picture
    already painted, one which had
        made us think of driving up to
            hairpin roads above the valley where branches
            snag like fishlines on the brushed
                surface of the

            river, so that we might look for
the church; a scene by a painter whose canvases
    are the size of an eyelid, who
        told us, "I have lived here now for
            years, but I've never entered the church.
            I don't need to, I can
                imagine it."

Skating in Harlem, Christmas Day

FOR MARY JO SALTER

Beyond the ice-bound stones and bucking trees,
past bewildered Mary, the Meer in snow,
two skating rinks and two black crooked paths

are a battered pair of reading glasses
scratched by the skater's multiplying math.
Beset, I play this game of tic-tac-toe.

Divide, subtract. Who can tell if love surpassses?
Two noughts we've learned make one astonished O—
a hectic night of goats and compasses.

Folly tells the truth by what it's not—
one X equals a fall I'd not forgo.
Are ice and fire the integers we've got?

Skating backwards tells another story—
the risky star above the freezing town,
a way to walk on water and not drown.

Primrose

All winter you kept yourself to yourself,
straitened, dumb, in the illegal fire escape
flower box; calyx, stem, sap, bud,

all at once and for all tucked in, spirit-flower
posthumously transferred from a florist's tub.
July, November, the strongbox snow discarded, your

ocelot's face marries the sun to itself, an orphan
Persephone, pulling herself hand over hand
from fire to fire, spring's last ember

the first conflagration of the earth returned,
the Primus stove lit, then out, then lit again
is her burning crown under the blue smoke of the trees.

The May Apple

Or mandrake. By the brook
I bent and parted the leaves.
Clefts. Veins. Smell

of musk, of mud. Tongue
slide of sap propelled,
shaking under the green.

Stung Io, her sentries
pale udder behind a bower—
day moon a white brow,

a chin sheer in water.
I wanted to put my face
to it, to its sheen

more animal than flower.

Fury

I saw Fury on the stair,
Beak in my heart,
But no one's there.
I saw Fury rattle a chair.
Crack in the mirror,
Cart drags the mare—
How does love stop?
How does it start?

I saw Fury all in satin.
"How can he love her?"
Asked the black wren.
"Sky fell down," said Mrs. Hen.
Where the crow flies
Is where it gets eaten—
Judge came back in
With a hung jury.

Black is the ribbon
On her nightgown.
Green the hangman
Who took her to town.
The table's set with fire,
Tears fill the tap—
Miracles happen
But not behind your back.

If I had a penny
Or a hundred or two,
I'd sail the world
Straight back to you.
The serpent eats a sparrow,

The wolf lies down—
Fury carries on
With a wheelbarrow.

Love blinks an eyelid,
Nothing is for sure.
Bang goes the hammer,
Echoes out the door.
Fury's whistling
The dead dark bright—
Hid star I wish
Upon the night.

Rotogravure

There was another life we knew each other
We were poor and hungry we lived in a palace
Cats supped in our place aloft we ate air
Trees were our nursemaids the moss sang to us
The door was heavy the reed gate was smashed
We drove through smoke we rode in carriages
We were far from the shore the ocean was near
The sky was jute the wet earth gray ash
We spoke in English in Russian we argued
The moon wore a mask the sun mirrored its moods
In the desert the thirsty went down to the water
Hummingbirds swarmed lions roared in quarries
Silence is an envelope noise is paper
This is a story poems come after stories

The Angel of the Resurrection

(FROM "PORT IMPERIAL")

Is it light on the trees
that turns them to pale fire
or is it spring, come without
    warning to this town on

stilts, set so precariously
above the river? All night my
heart is an owl perched on
    a high branch, its feathers

ablaze, its question answered
by the face of the Angel
of the Resurrection, reflected
    in water as your hand

prints itself on my bones,
head bowed, mouth an O,
burning, drinking the river
    in order to breathe.

Heirloom

"Take it," my grandmother said. "You
    might as well have it now."
"No," I said, knowing what now meant.
    But I took it anyway, when
I left, leaving a white space   —
    a window where the picture went.

I brought it home and hung it up:
    my grandmother, young, reading
under some trees. Red dress and shoes,
    the same rooster red used, for
effect, on a rooftop skirting
    a broad, heavy sky of news-

paper gray, her wide book a pair
    of white goose wings, shedding
light on her face. What is happening
    in those pages? She doesn't
look up, there's no hint of the artist,
    my grandfather, dampening

his brushes a few yards away,
    about as far as I sit
from her now, although to me,
    at this distance, she's a good
deal smaller—a painted figure
    in a painting. A tree

is a waterspout, a peaked roof
    is a bird, a frill of roses verges

on a lilac hedge. And the orangerie
in back—a fantasy? A hotel?
He's painted the frame the exact shade
of the sky, wet streaks of greeny-

gray, as though if he just pushed out
the margin far enough, the packed
clouds might hold off forever. But
when the storm starts, won't they pack
up, go in? Barbed lightning might hurl
tridents on the uncut

lawn; my grandfather would have
closed his easel, my grandmother
her book. Or did she read on, staying
in the rain until the last
word of the chapter, a phrase so
long, it unwinds here, a fraying

wire that holds up a second picture
painted by the same hand,
fluent, now, on a matching square
of bristol board. It's late in the day.
Across a green smear of fields
a river swells to an inlet where

two children, poles taut in their hands,
are fishing. The boy is my father,
the girl, my aunt. On the surface
of the water the painter has drawn
himself in as a shadow, but what
he sees, we see: the open field

suffused with sun, the runnels stoked
with darkness, the boy's smoke-swirl

of hair; twilight, the day receding,
    the girl's red dress an old one
cut down, as if this was the story
    my grandmother is so endlessly reading.

Another Snowman

Lacy eyelet, and dark patches
of snowmelt, and paper snowflakes—

sharp as the bottle green leaves of
the blackthorn hedge. Outside, alone

beneath the frozen tulip tree's
long limbs, a child builds a snowman

out of drifts. But what will he eat?
What will he wear? A hickory

stick. A hat, brand-new. "Who are you?"
asks the child. "I am the cold," he

says, "that you let live." She does his
charcoal buttons, snug and tight. Snow

falls. The afternoon spins. "What time
has wrought," the dream says, "I let in."

Lasting is hard. Too hard at last.
In love she holds the snowman's hand.

Spell

Black wick, singed, that means to burn,
     drowning water, where the dry-eyed sun
drags its gaze along disastrous stones,
     fish bone, cold ground, malevolent leaf,
our gravity that leads us all to grief,
     to you, who watched me write this down:
while I am on this earth, and then after—
     where she will be, let breath be found.

Round for a Plague Year

In time remote from this new time
in brightness underneath the trees,
you laugh and cast your shadow down
in petals falling thick and fast.

Around a name we make a rhyme.
White bone and dust, blossom and ash—
we make as we will to the last
our shadows rhyme with dust and dance.

In time remote from this new time,
in dry grass underneath the trees,
a darning needle's silver flash—
spindle, plague, blossom, dance:

a blackened shadow hurrying past,
in burnt leaves falling thick and fast.
Waving now, you clap your hands,
bright petal turned to dust and ash.

Michael's Boat

When at night you woke
I sang to you, light in my arms
and your cheek wet, and the shore
    we rowed toward was sleep.

Two a.m., four a.m.,
the sky brightening, our passage
abandoned as the last star
    to steer by faded. Milk

and honey, trumpet vine,
the hours swelling in the thick
June heat as I crossed the wide
    floorboards, singing

the only song that
settled you, as if you knew
even then the journey we were on,
    that we were leaving, or

that I was, and you
would be forever heading into
open water, past gray shallows
    where the wrecked ship

molts, splintering
at the high-water line, turning
from boat to felled kite:
    a boat whose rigging

should have let it
fly, but which withered instead

like the willow judged by
   Michael, "Let the Lord

rebuke you." Shadow.
Inland. Four, five, six summers
pass. Too heavy now to carry
   when you stir, you rise

instead, and walk,
somnambulist, around the room.
I sit up late. Asleep, you
   seem to know your way.

Porpoise who swims
in the watercourse we made, I stand
on grief's upper deck and hear
   you ask, in the silence

of the song's long
shade, "Whose boat is it, anyway?"
"It is yours," I think, but
   do not answer.

Custody

A telephone rings in the vast house.
No shadow to the far-off sound,
but here dark gathers in high clouds,
as if the earth had spun around,
and through a telescope I see
the moon's cold cheek beset by storms,
black sky that cannot, will not pass,
carbon in sunlight's marigold.

My child is gone too far from me.
She is too fair, too wise, too old.
With every greeting she departs,
she goes to where I cannot go.
I know it, though—the logs are lit,
the beach fills up with party guests.
Ankle-deep, she stands in surf,
sand holding her as I cannot.

It's better than it could have been,
by far, since what once was turned out
to be some other way, and all
is well except it never ends.
Waves hug the shore with their long shrug—
the riptide that was out is in.
She moves to speak, I tilt the lens.
Soon this view will grow cold too.

Auden in the Aquarium

It was a hot day in June.
Inside the aquarium it was so cool
after the bright light outside that
it seemed as if we were swimming up
the arteries of a cold broad-backed fish.

We took in the crabs, the sea urchins,
the jellyfish that shone like
Japanese lanterns, and as we looked
our reflections flitted past us
on the green grass, animated, lit,

as if this was the shade to which
they are always hoping to return,
the reason they only show themselves
on surfaces that mimic water.
At some of the tanks the lights

had been arranged so there were
no reflections—it was like looking
through a window with the sash
raised—and it was at one of these
I saw you, Wystan, your crepe-paper

face on a huge tautog, swimming alone
in a clutch of striped bass.
The bass kept opening and shutting
their mouths like sheep, or choristers
—though their singing was completely

inaudible—and along their sides
were dark inky lines, like the marks

of tire tracks. There was an eel
there too, below you, its body
an S, then an O, at home, at least

it seemed, in its permanently
unitarian element: air filtered, fire
tamped down. The aquarium was filled
with schoolchildren, whistling,
shoving, with tourists in their

tropical clothes, waiting, as we were,
for the ferry to Vineyard Haven.
We stood at the tank. The glass was cold.
A tent of light shone down. Your scales
were the color of old silver, of smoke.

Behind you on the wall were a few
artfully painted sea grasses,
a few rocks, a wave but no sign
of a boy, and a warning:
    DO NOT TAP ON GLASS
for you to read backwards, in Icelandic.

A Sighting

Another anniversary of your death.
A few of us, by coincidence,
are at the skating rink again,

this time, to be sure,
with infants in tow.
From the side I watch you dip and glide,

dear wraith among the figure eights.

I want to call to you but know I can't.
The air is cold, I catch my breath.
The child I'm watching hugs the edge,

until you who are each death this decade brought,
swoop close to guide him toward the fray,
and then return to where it was you came from,

saving a place for us,
who will in turn save one for him.

Rocking the Carriage

FOR ANNA

For years we kept one in the hall
and rocked the baby there to sleep,
up and down the long dim corridor.
It was a job that someone had,
laundry half folded, papers unread.
Somewhere there was always fog
or snow, or so the radio said.
Rocking went on right through the zones,
past reckonings and acts of God.
So little happened in the hall
—the odd leak, a warped door not shut—
that often, lulled, I couldn't tell,
the child I wanted so to sleep,
was it Jack, Beatrice, or Rose?
The carriage wheels had turned so long
they wore a track into the floor,
and some days as I stood and pushed,
the pictures on the painted walls
were windows, and the hall, a train,
and down the railroad ties we rode,
past sunsets, cows, past bicyclists,
past towns. I liked a neon sign
that advertised an old racetrack.
Bright red, the horse and rider moved.
A clock. A steeple. Another train
charged backwards with a hiss.
We stopped once, halting sharply, to
let others in: an aged aunt,
a friend, just dead. Sandwiches were fetched.
My friend took out a book to read,
but though I tried, I couldn't see
the spine. (She couldn't answer, so

I didn't ask.) When lunch was done,
a girl got up to say good-bye.
"Oh look," I said, "you're all grown up."
She wasn't hard to recognize.
Her face grew small until, a cloud,
it rose above a pinafore.
"See you," she said. Then one by one,
the rest got on and off, as if she,
being the eldest, had shown them how.

The train passed through a clear cold night.
Trees were met once, the moon many times.
Hills undulated out of sight
as if the dreaming earth had stirred,
or a giant tossed a blanket down.
Then the view changed. A stony place
stretched out as far as I could see,
the distance held by a green maze
whose branches met above my head.
"Ssh," I said. "The baby mustn't wake."
With one hand I reached up and touched
the emerald mat of prickly leaves,
no hedge now, but a loose tweed sleeve
which I clutched hard so not to fall.
My step made bigger to match hers,
I swayed as if I walked between
two railway cars about to part.

And with my other hand I rocked
the grizzling baby in the hall,
willing no noise to break the spell—
the downstairs bell, a caterwaul,
a crying child, a train whistle.

from

THE ADA POEMS

(2010)

Birch

Bone-spur, stirrup of veins—white colt
a tree, sapling bone again, worn to a splinter,
    a steeple, the birch aground

in its ravine of leaves. Abide with me, arrive
at its skinned branches, its arms pulled
    from the sapling, your wrist taut,

each ganglion a gash in the tree's rent
trunk, a child's hackwork, *love plus love,*
    my palms in your fist, that

trio a trident splitting the birch, its bark
papyrus, its scars calligraphy,
    a ghost story written on

winding sheets, the trunk bowing, *dead is
my father,* the birch reading the news
    of the day aloud as if we hadn't

heard it, the root moss lit gas,
like the veins on your ink-stained hand—
    the birch all elbows, taking us in.

Aesop

"'Our black rainbow,' Ada termed it, '... inside a grille of rain.'"

Cold on each leaf, cut glass, cold where you are—
at dawn my palms cross-hatched by tiny cuts
as if sharp-beaked birds had tried to eat but
finding nothing pecked instead. What knock-kneed
gentled monkey salves and holds the cat's
burnt paw? Nothing makes this right but that it
is—wild for twenty years, in Ektachrome,
you've buttoned your old jacket wrong; the cast
die said you can't redo it, or this, or
graze from my hand. Chastened, what can we do
but mutter, talk, and read? Dear heart, the years
caught up with us. Like tortoises, they've passed
the too-sure hare, and racing, gone ahead—
daring us—posthumous—to live on air.

Regime

Two days of no word—or three—I imagine
Pound's letter, the cold blue plums—Imogene
cast out; her card marked: death by fen, by fire.
Mute, woe woos both beggar-maid and chooser
but my woe is marriage. We balk and shy.
Your voice is gravel, chalk, convoking star.
I wake to dream. You who are not here—not
here. How far would I come to meet you?
The road is thick with snow, the river black ice—
in your father's clothes you turn to smoke, then
skywriting. This fall, driving north, and north—
the shaken world awash, myrmidon, swot
ambergris—the fierce trees with their platelet
streams, each leaf a handprint, corporeal.

First Dreamscape

No one but lovers and children tell their dreams:
not fish, nearer fowl, where does that leave me—
bantam in the barnyard, pecking for mash.
Bleak lovebirds, our nests are spangled with remorse
and love; for us the order out of kilter:
what we love, we burn. In the dream, Devon,
Kentisbeare, winter, but the lawns still
green, the stone church black with wet against
the brackish sky, the mourners quickly off
in twos and threes—abashed at talking yet
they still went on. I was the dreamer—dead,
I had to choose. The scene tilted. The emerald
air was now the scuffed mill's cuckoo cloud.
Twice shy. I'd never left except with you.

Christmas I

"She was on bad terms with memory."

No longer able to think or write or breathe—
New York a cynosure of drink and guilt,
the sweetheart roses tilt their faces
to the piano's black sateen bat wing.
Before the shoe is thrown and King Rat falls,
there's Queen Victoria in bombazine,
a bleary tear sheet bunched to feed the flames.
I sit on the stairs and stare. The snapdragons
open their pale throats to sneeze—chrysanthemum
smell of burning hair. Below, our old tortoise
paces the scorched carpet. On his armoured back
a sparkler shooting red and green. One letter
less, *amour* is his world. Whose name is Mother?
I hardly know my hand that struck the match.

Second Dreamscape (New Year's Night)

The road we walked in winter was a figure eight.
In the cabin, Möbius's flypaper strip dangled
from the ceiling, its amber isinglass. Pines
pressed in, fish bones, quill scales dead upright
—a feather headdress, finished here and there
with diamond filigree—and the ceiling was the sky,
a snow globe where it kept snowing
on the covered bridge, and the barn,
and the moon rose like a quarter but shone
only if you could guess—*heads or tails*—
but even if the man in the moon wouldn't speak
and turned his back and put on his hat
light shone anyway on his white hair
and we walked and walked until the hemisphere
split like an orange, and we were back
inside. It was very late. The strip
had caught more flies than we could count
and a spider too, a miniature miracle,
all legs and eyes, and the green feathers
were still dipped in snow.

New Mexico/Sangre de Cristo Mountains/Epiphany

". . . a tiny theater that specialized in Painted Westerns."

The fir trees Russian in their tulle of snow,
their children ravens in hemstitched chemises
allowed up late to see the Kings.
At Jemez Pueblo, boys at once too young,
too old, their ladder Jacob's own beneath
the cow-faced clouds, pretend to fly and fall,
then catch themselves, until the blue-faced
buffalos—their uncles—make them stop
and stare. I never thought you couldn't take
care of—*fill in the blanks.* Why can't I want
anything I want? Drumbeats. Caws. And though
we asked and asked, no one could tell us where
the Madonna was, our breath resin, the mist
a houri hired by the hour to ogle the moon.

Letter

Older, slyer. Silence spent, for days we've
sped and shied. My country stands and falls
with and without you—last night cop cars,
sharks outside the house; scenting fear, they have
no choice but to school and whir. Nothing
tears me from blood sport, ganglia singing—
sand under my spine and you intent, a boy
hearing his own name as birdsong, counting
my pulse, a tern darting. Daedalus, whose
spokes set the sea afire—nothing we kept
did anything but burn, each hair singed by
the cigarette's acrid kiss. Needle bent,
my rattletrap compass shuns the North Star's pull;
your wet hand stung by the eel's charged swerve.

Letter Two

"'Destroy and forget,' said Ada."

Lost ring, lost shoe, lost fortune, fortune found—
what blessing is a burden when its head is turned?
The Jack of Spades become the Suicide King,
loss by way of love and lose. Bee sting.
The mind swells, ricochets until every card
has your face. The black cat's languor, snarled
as yarn, turns into morning's yawning hall
of mirrors. Do you remember our walks
along the Hudson, the trashed seventies washing up,
girding the houseboats with gilt flotsam?
Fervent croupier, all hands and eyes, your
mascara an inked gate that would slam down—
blame is Gilead's crop, he jokes for food.
I'd trade every moment for any moment.

Monday Rhyme (Khartoum)

"Oh, write me, one tiny note . . . ?"

I love you in the desert
I love you by the shore
My love for you is a windward ship
How could I ask for more?

It flies across the continents
Bold frigate, carpet, centaur
Brash rainbow studded with sylvan bells—
Why would I ask for more?

Love, the years are legion
The past was white and noir
You were on the snow-lashed steppes—
I fished without a lure.

Now the moon has rattled
The starry dipper poured—
If years mean far from where you are
I stop at any more.

Greek Poem

You came out of winter
    approaching.
Death and more death
    and my heart was
cold to you.

You said:
    talk to me.
I was
    a stone
thrown in the river.

We spoke. We were
    as children, speaking.
Then not—
      my head bent back.

Not quiet.

    *

—quick fish—scales—lapis—
    child practicing scales—

    *

You asked me to come
     and I did.

   Where were you?
you asked, if I slept.

. . .

And then you took
   out your stock

of silence, those thick
   dry goods.

You are a managing director
   of silence.

I should have
known
   that silence

anywhere.

And I should not
     have listened to you
at the river.

But I was happy
   to hear your
voice again—

the sound
   of my heart beating.

It is my own fault
     that I listened

       to you, to that
          lyre in the reeds.

Aubade Against Grief

Chaste sun who would not light your face
pale as the fates
   who vanished

when we turned aside; recluse
whom grace
   returned and by returning banished

all thought but: Love, late
sleeper in the early hours, flesh of my bone,
   centaur: Excuse

my faults—tardiness, obtuse
remit of my own
   heart, unruly haste

to keep my mouth on yours, to wipe the slate
clean, to atone—
   what could I want but to wait

for that light to touch your face,
chaste as Eros in the first wished-
   on rush of wings?

Spring Thaw

"... that tattered chapbook ..."

My left hand has never known my right.
The tinderbox it keeps to strike

the matchstick house my right hand built
by drawing and redrawing lines

like someone who can't love or learn
or read the reeling smoke's too-likely scrawl.

I wrote that, too, above the house I drew.
Can't, or won't. My heart's not right.

My right hand saves what my left burns
as if what's left—that black cloud, those few

reticulate, neglected trees—could be kept
where everything but what you want is free.

To draw a circus tent, and not a house!
As if I could—velvet swags, a white

cat whose kittens are bows on a kite
string, a solitary dog, hermaphrodite

who loves himself both day and night.
(His? her? pinhole-parasol lets teardrops fall.)

Let's stop—*no*—and name him Aphrodite.
I could go on and on, being free—

freehand, that is. But I wish I'd known
earlier how it would feel, what might

. . .

go wrong, what hurt, what didn't, after all.
Or if the two-stroke charcoal roof could bear

a row of exponential birds in azure air.

April (Aboard the Half Moon*)*

The minutes rickshaws strung with fairy lights—
better just to read and gaze, the river slips,
amethyst to tourmaline, lapping—
            interrupt, interrupt, rip up, rip up—:
    late, *I couldn't wake to catch a plane.*
The clock ticked fourteen over Westbourne Grove—
    the paintbrush irises were second hands.
In the junkshop, King Edward's valet's sofa,
tattered mauve, held court beneath a vale
of crystal tears. Do you remember the wolf
who baited shadow rabbits on the wall
of our West End Avenue fourth-story dive?
He was too dear and ragged to leave home.

This in magic marker on a paper plate.

Poem for a Printing Press

FOR NICHOLAS MCBURNEY

". . . dubious words in a number of lexicons [. . .]"

A is for angel
　　　B is for bone
C is a carillon
　　　D is a doe
　E isn't easy
　　F wants to fly
G is for gee whiz
　　　H says hiss
I is for impulse
　　　J is for jewel
K is a kitty hawk
　　　L is for lose
M sends a message
　　　　N says no
　P is the piper
　　　Q calls it quits
　R is for red
　　　S is the snake
T is for troubles
　　U stays up late
V is for vanquish
　　W asks why
X is an answer
　　　Y is for yes
　　　Z is for zed

　But wait—
　　　O—*oh*—rolled away.

Electric Light

"('True, my lovely and larveless.')"

The dragonfly whirs and whirs and will not stop
replaying its ceaseless hum over the tightly pulled rungs
of wire at the topmost end of the scale.
Fire runs along the wires as if someone had wrapped
the sound in rags and lit a match. St. George
in his emerald livery, his tiny jeweled sword drawn, has no time
　　for this domestic crisis, more darning needle
than dragon, who with ragged black stitches tries
to sew up the seam while busily sawing the air
　　　with its tarnished wings
but the tear is there.
Through it I see the blue scribbled-on sky over the sea
where a quiver of dragonflies draws frantic lines
over the high weed-choked rocky dunes.
It wasn't this summer, I don't think so, but the summer before last.
Hot, glassine—no one
knew why they had come nor why were there so many of
　　them—obviously speaking
to each other in a language made up of static
fueled by the sun, the sound of steel wool
on a washboard, filling the space between earth
and air by writing over and over it,
　　　　as my hand does here
—if only one could swallow the sword and be done with it—
leaving no place, under the din of the white-hot filament
of the reading light, free of your name.

Third Dreamscape

"There are people who can fold a road map."

I NEW AMSTERDAM–COLRAIN

The rain all night made rivulets in the garden
between the flagstones and the ferns, which were
just starting to unfold their fan fronds underneath
the sky's turned-down indigo cup. The rain broke up
the earth into islands and promontories flecked
here and there with green—moss, I think, though it's
too early and too cold. Rain raced down the window,
a no-legged race played out to nothing.
The tears behind my lids are more fire than water.
What does the fire say? Black heart, white ash.
Outside, the mocking bird hoots
but does not answer. Hecuba, barking.
Your sure hand in the dog's fur. Too early. You're sleeping too.
It's snowing where you are. The dark-rimmed dog's eye
is the sun behind a raindrop, an eclipse, a peeled rind.

II ORVIETO

It wasn't Ravenna, it was—I had to look it up
in the bookcase under the stairs, in the blue guidebook—
I was looking for a place to buy a shoelace, apparently,
in 1980. There it is, carefully written out, *merletti.*
The corner turned down, the penciled circle smeared
to a rain cloud: how strange rereading doesn't wear
print off the page.
          Could it be there still, the shop
with its row of priests' shoes, tongues barely
bound by the gnarled laces?
A pair of gold evening slippers was strung up in the window

next to a dried palm cross. (One tongue is Hecuba's,
thumping her tail in the dream.)
And the slippers, who lost them, or bought them?
Hazelnut, chocolate, strawberry, tiramisu—at the *gelataria*
the ices were set in a compass wheel
under the counter, a frozen scoop marking every direction on earth,
the last, blood orange, set in a hollowed-out rind threaded
with white capillaries,
                    a pink emergency,
and in the piazza, the black-and-white cathedral, built
to commemorate the miracle at Bolzano, six
kilometers away, when blood dripped from an altar cloth
"and convinced the priest of the Real Presence,"
rose straight up like a Sunday hat, with a black-
and-white striped ribbon woven through
the intricate herringbone straw-colored brick.
Or a herd of zebras, all eyes and legs and hide.
Inside the chapel, on the long south wall, angels guided
The Blessed to Paradise (the fresco was especially lurid,
as if light couldn't be anything but blinding) and beyond them
was the same hillside we had seen outside,
winding up to that very spot,
which as I remember it
was covered with poppies.
Red, red everywhere: the poppies, the altar cloth, the red stripe
of paint that marks the collar of the brown dog who darts
at Dante's feet in the fresco as he watches the pilgrimage—
a pearl necklace of souls spiraling to heaven.
The front of the cathedral, the side facing the piazza,
was bandaged with drop cloths and struts of scaffolding.
The repairs must be finished now, or begun again.
What were we doing there, in Orvieto, looking
and looking until we were dizzy? Who, even
then, was *we,* and who was *I,* that *I* that was heading
towards you, now that once again

one instant of your gray gaze has smote
the barking dog, the scudding rain,
the piazza, turning them ghostly as if they never were?
Striped cool fell on my bare arms and legs
in a grotto of shade beside the cathedral.
The ice cream tasted faintly of grass
and was cold on my tongue as last night

before the rain started, holding a cold glass of green wine
labeled Orvieto, I looked at a row of books and couldn't remember
which page held the scene I was looking for—
the black-and-white shadow of the balustrade in an old house,
the dog begging scraps from the table
and two people on the landing who pulled away
from each other a moment too soon, that flick of the curtain
a teardrop, eyelet along the sill
caught but fluttering—

III   RAVENNA–COLRAIN

the way the dove in the fountain in Ravenna, where I went
the next week (each inch of her a separate glittering stone)
held her wings open in the water in the basin
where the hairlines of mortar were studded
with viridian moss, a few tiny angel wings unfolding
now that the ice is broken—the dog out for a walk
pausing to drink, shaking his fur as he lifts his head
each drop mercurial, a convex mirror, an open eye
silver against the fountain's upturned dark blue stone cup.

Hermes, 1981

Bird bones barely hardened, a river
of blue vein, hyacinth blue, you
reached for the lintel—if desire
were meat I would hold that moment
        forever in my mouth.

Late Poem

"... a matter of changing a slide in a magic lantern."

I wish we were Indians and ate foie gras
and drove a gas-guzzler
and never wore seat belts

I'd have a baby, yours, *cette fois,*
and I'd smoke Parliaments
and we'd drink our way through the winter

in spring the baby would laugh at the moon
who is her father and her mother who is his pool
and we'd walk backwards and forwards

in lizard-skin cowboy boots
and read *Gilgamesh* and *Tintin* aloud
I'd wear only leather or feathers

plucked from endangered birds and silk
from exploited silkworms
we'd read *The Economist*

it would be before and after the internet
I'd send you letters by carrier pigeons
who would only fly from one window

to another in our drafty, gigantic house
with twenty-three uninsulated windows
and the dog would be always

off his leash and always
find his way home as we will one day
and we'd feed small children

. . .

peanut butter and coffee in their milk
and I'd keep my hand glued under your belt
even while driving and cooking

and no one would have our number
except I would have yours where I've kept it
carved on the sole of my stiletto

which I would always wear when we walked
in the frozen and dusty wood
and we would keep warm by bickering

and falling into bed perpetually and
entirely unsafely as all the best things are
—your skin and my breath on it.

Old-Fashioned Poem

The truth is I always think of you.
The garden is beautiful as a folktale—
speedwell, oxalis, and foxglove,
white moths above the foamflower.
What would it be like I wonder
    if want were set as song,
to sit with you in the evening, my life's love,
as cats eye bees in the bee balm
and the shade grows long?

Fugue: Pilgrim Valley

Again I find myself in tears—find myself,
that lost one—asleep at noon beneath
the gazebo's furrowed brow. Yesterday
I took the ferry and drove south inside
summer's buzzing gong: Clotho, a spider
letting her silk pulley down along each
capillary lane, stippled with tiger lilies,
their garnet throats rimmed with kohl above wild
carrot ruffs, a bleached galaxy—Queen Anne's
openwork plied to make heads turn. The past's
clear colors make the future dim, Lethe's
swale laced with willow twigs. Nothing happened
without you. I want you to see what I see—
I'm talking with your fingers caught in my mouth.

From The Book of Knowledge

(*THE CHILDREN'S ENCYCLOPEDIA* / THE GROLIER SOCIETY, VOL. 115, 1936)

"For the snake of a rhyme," cried Ada.

FOR KATHERINE AND BENJAMIN SWETT

1. What makes a fairy ring?
   Fairy rings are made of a kind of fungus.

2. Why does damp air make us ill?
   Damp air is often cold air, and the cold has usually been blamed for making us ill, though many facts prove that it is not blameworthy at all.

3. Why does a dog go round and round before it lies down?
   The answer to this question lies in another question. What is a dog?

4. Can our brains ever fill up?
   The poet Browning says "there is no end to learning."

5. Why does a tuning fork sound louder when it touches wood?
   The sound from a tuning fork, like the light from a candle, flows out in all directions.

6. Why are some things poisonous?
   We could only answer this question completely and fully if we knew all there is to know about life.

7. Why can we hear better when we shut our eyes?
   This question is partly true and partly not true.

8. Can an animal think?
   There is no doubt an animal can think, and that it can remember.

9. Do animals feel pain as we do?
That is not a question that can be answered directly.

10. Why do we not growl like animals when we are hungry?
A hungry man is an angry man.

11. Why have leaves different shapes?
The great idea which we learn to apply to every fact about living creatures is that these facts usually have uses.

12. Why do the leaves of the aspen always shake?
The shaking of the leaves has the same effect as if the trees were fanning themselves.

13. Why does oil make a wheel go round more easily?
It all depends on where the oil is put.

14. Why do we see the stars only at night?
The stars are shining all the time, sending light to earth, but more than this is needed for us to see.

15. Is an atom alive?
It is almost a living thing.

16. Can country people see "writ small" better than townspeople?
If country folk use their eyes mainly at distances, their vision will be keenest at distances.

17. Why does a lump rise in my throat when I cry?
It is the place of speech which is the most marvelous thing.

At Cow Hollow

The bay is watered silk, then convex, a mirror
holding a clutch of sleepers, brown-eyed pansies,
their irises topaz, planetary.
I wonder if you think of me. Rain at dawn;
at dusk, the water crepe de chine, the sky
reversed: washed minarets, the urchins' pinchbeck
turbans strewn to dry. In New York, our local
seeress, Madam Amphitrite, hangs
out her shingle: *By Appointment Only,*
Two to Four. Left on my own five minutes,
I don't know whether to weep or sleep.
The life I have without you goes on without me—
far out, a catboat locked in rainbow haze.
Moths shatter the sun with their burnt wings.

At Sunflower Farm

"(Ada: 'They are now practically extinct at Ardis.')"

Instead of Cyclops' eye, the phoenix, infra-
red: Sebastian's gold ring in his mouth,
his herded arrows silver birds, their wings
tipped with poisoned wood. When Solzhenitsyn
moved to Pomfret his neighbors posted signs:
NO DIRECTIONS TO THE SOLZHENITSYNS.
Dead, since we've spoken. Crab-claw of ice, when
Cúchulain slew the waves he knew he'd lost.
Each wrong I do rescores my palm's triplet
life line. Entrails, outmoded—my played-out
pride, like pot or protest; the Anglo-Saxon
that we learned lockstep taught us fate not choice.
Love, look: the bronze sunflower whose seed face
scatters without the seed tearing apart.

Irish Poem

I looked for want
and want I found
where'er I went
over blent ground
my heart I stilled
my ear I bent
but not a word
or sound I heard.

I looked for want
dumb heart in two
no sound or word
but what I found
was what it meant—
where'er I went
I could not find
my own blind bird.

I looked for want
where'er I went
with my heart rent
and what I found
was bone split too—
a raven's nest
my eye did find
and a bird blind.

My heart in two
was my own heart
the coal black bird
was my own ear
that heard no sound

nor would come near
that song too dear
for me to hear.

I looked for want
and want I found
my name is want
no song, no sound
the whitened ground
is where I went
I took my heart
where the road bent.

Now hare, my heart
I say to you
what is the sound
that these bones meant
to play upon
the trees' bent boughs?
In accident
the song did start—

where the road bent
my heart did part.
I looked for want
and want I found—
I wanted want
for I was meant
to hear the sound
of what I heard
since love did start.

Coda

These fitful poems are our daft child—
first wonder, faith's blue eye, the green-blue planet's almost haze
    that lifts, clouds' gauze and lingering storm shade

        then fists beating, half merman,
    half wraith, a leaping herring
wrapped in newsprint's thrice-printed ink—
        that plaided quarto, is your gift, and mine.
    The icon, that cast die, and not ever once being warm
           so looking for warmth, that tartan

        a green copse, re-crossed with Chinese red,
           its runnels watered blood—the poet dipped
           his pen in water twice

    so the fawn, its fur spattered with blurred stars
           won't turn and bolt
but stay fast, indefinitely—
        gaze fixed by the headlight's hazel.

Pine tree in snow, the bled herringbone's woven spire
    its star reading the wood's tea leaves,

what makes the hunter dear and the deer the hunter?
    Love must be put
into action—this is the action.

from

ORBIT

(2017)

Flowers

This morning I was walking upstairs
from the kitchen, carrying your
beautiful flowers, the flowers you

brought me last night, calla lilies
and something else, I am not
sure what to call them, white flowers,

of course you had no way of knowing
it has been years since I bought
white flowers—but now you have

and here they are again. I was carrying
your flowers and a coffee cup
and a soft yellow handbag and a book

of poems by a Chinese poet, in
which I had just read the words "come
or go but don't just stand there

in the doorway," as usual I was
carrying too many things, you
would have laughed if you saw me.

It seemed especially important
not to spill the coffee as I usually
do, as I turned up the stairs,

inside the whorl of the house as if
I were walking up inside the lilies.
I do not know how to hold all

the beauty and sorrow of my life.

Meltwater

A gang of foxes on the wet road, fur
gaggle, the gutter a Ganges, gravel
rutting the glacier's slur and cant. Old proof,
the past can't solve itself, endlessly drawing
its stung logos spirograph. You see
the fox I cannot see; even the children
can see her, vixen and her babies
delicately picking their way along
the white line of the tarmac, the rain
rubbing out their shadows. I want you
as I want water, rain crocheting moss
from mist, sulfur on the pines' crooked limbs,
hapless as the selkie who hums to herself—
no one believes in her but there she is.

Faun

The faun you can see
    her lariat of bone unfolding

the faun in your arms
    her legs buckled

      moon-mouth

velvet, her breath keyed,
    water

    rasping the bridge
barnacles ringing the pilings
    —black pearls,

the faun's breath spiral,
    circling your head,
    the Horn of Africa

      pausing
—digitalis,
    cinquefoil, starburst

    pulsing
    to where we walked

    to the end, to what we
thought was the end.

Orbit

je vais voir l'ombre que tu devins
—MALLARMÉ

That evening when you were standing by
the shelves and song came back to you after
a long silence, never broken even once
but for a shadow crossing your path, a murmur
of some long-ago breath, speeches as nursery rhymes,
St. Crispin or the children chanting, *please you,*
night and day, or the stained glass of the bay
as it opened for you when the tide rose
to meet the twilight. But never asking for you,
who had become a bystander, salt caked
by salt to a pillar and even then slipshod
with the truth. That swerving eel whose charge switches
the current is you, not another, slick
tail—remorse—caught in its own mouth.

*

The house a shell and not a shell. Dreaming,
I stop at each turn of the stair, kite
winder, the balustrade's tipped ladder tracking
infinity, each door a lid shut tight,
my damp snail foot, proboscis, wrack fishtail.
How can I swim up so many stories?
On the landing, furs. Gloves. A walking stick,
Grandfather in his overcoat, clearing
his throat, the winter smell of carnations.
I tried to write it down but lost. Missed tread.
Footfall of what the dead said. Don't, or do?
All ear, I have no hands. Lunatic hero,
the hermit crab who keeps me company
turns me over, nebulae, on my back.

All day a playing card at the kitchen stair's hairpin,
seven diamonds, each red gem a step, Mnemosyne's
daughters, sun-sprockets, whirring to make you *listen*.
On a sequined pillow from Bombay, our Una's
papoose doll sits up beneath *The Book
of Justice,* a pop-up fugue whose page unfolds
a toothpick temple, each strut a reliquary,
its cellophane banner sheer petroleum.
By midnight, the card picked up: tears, doom-bringer,
futility: the owl asking its question
to the barking of dogs. Rusks and cardamom.
If Chronos comes to Hecate's door, what use
is squabbling? Yew-eyed, the cat mews the stair,
her footprints red after she steps on glass.

*

Dusk. Bee's *Sea of Monsters* butts the chair—
its shiny cover wreathed with lashing tails
while eight steps up, the kite winder, littered
with gilt ribbons, sails into Whitehall's helter-
skelter. I sit "on the stares." Fight or flight?
Downstairs, on pink ice, powdered ginger
spackles the Victorian mold's flutes with gold,
red lily pollen, prodded, makes us all
Macbeth. Tonight's story? Trawling for loot,
wan Elnora, *"A Girl of the Limberlost,"*
pulls from her torn pocket a scrimshaw boy,
a locket, a painted top—each butterfly
she nets a flustered treble note. We're not
good at being good, nor being *"good-at."*

The fireplace log breathes fire, pooled amber,
bejeweled topaz lighting a goblet. The air
is sap. Dragon, the pine log shatters to
a monkey face, two knots for eyes, then—gone.
What else eats itself alive? The child, not
eating, rattles her shark spine, wind chimes
for Belsen's banging door that only shuts.
North, the smudged mill towns carbonize, each one
dilated, black iris beneath the day's
cloud-muddied brow, horizon's dorsal fin
snow grey, as if the flooded dawn held dusk,
the shark's inamorata sunset's skinned
knuckle try at holding fast—gunpowder
sky that drinks smoke from an hourglass.

*

Each one Echo (spitting image of Narcissus
in diminuendo), the seven sisters play
bridge on their upside-down card table,
their meteor go-cart running on a firecracker.
Their swaged tablecloth is the snow sky settling
on the dark town. Who could do wrong? The eye
of the world opens and shuts. Remember
the legs under the table, silk and suede,
pine bark, sharp hooves, clattering? We spoke
in whispers, hardly breathing—house of cards
where every breath disturbs the dreaming portraits.
Shuffle the deck. The prince's tiny twitching
dog is dreaming us: dust and ore, secret, alive,
animal, just past vision's humming line.

*

Why can't I want anything I want? But,
Cosmo, I do. Posthumous, our loves
outlive us: hardtack, lemons, sassafras,
soap-skiff floating in the clawfoot tub,
the windlass a girl blowing bubbles.
Would that we'd known? A whitened cloud
of peppered moths, the children's old *de teum*
dims the lamp, singes the too-light evening
and turns the sky's slashed moiré tangerine.
I bartered forty summers for black pearls—
the cat's black tail, scorch mark, rounds the kicked
shut door. On Wings Neck two deer eat and graze.
I slip and water slops the stairs. Where I am
met is meat. What we knew we know was there.

*

The light through the wicker chair makes star-crossed
diamonds on the coffee cup, each watery
crystal quartz alit tells lies or makes
things up. What will I do with my life?
Rolled up the map of Angers—*somewhere else*—
resists, its antique blue print paper folds
an origami house on fire, its routes
and rivers set ablaze, the blown up center—
court, steeple, winding stair—a burnt out
    charcoal spyhole. Between the lines? In
the kitchen of the dragon king, the hooked carp,
speaking, has one wish: life as we know it.
Know-nothing, the curling paper serpent
sheds his printed skin but leaves me mine.

Tea-smoked duck on a sugar stick, at
the restaurant where in the dream I changed
tables and changed tables. Everything M. gave me
was a box—a glass box with pink transparent sides,
        a cloisonné *parfumerie.*
Do you want these boots? the dream said. I walked for miles
through racks of shoes, among the voodoo dolls—
but those are Martin's, I said. But who is Martin?
Then woke—*I am half turned away*—to rain,
and didn't think, a meal half-cooked, the stove aflame,
duck legs puckered running red, the cat left out all night
drenched and I—*you don't think,* who have failed
everyone I love, my hair a fright wig
        my heart a bat that bangs its head.

    *

Shellacked with ice, the street a cracked snow globe
whose magic pool drips serum. Mystery or venom?
Reading aloud in our cocoa-cum-coffee cloud,
Miss Stanton, stepdaughter of Woking, Surrey,
drops her veil. It's not sorrow she feels, but terror,
then comedy—the bull butting his maze
of twigs, the baboon rattling the bedroom door.
Is love labor? *Pacem,* heart-ease. Our shadows
slip. In the ashram's hand-thrown toffee bowl
(our guru has a sweet tooth, he likes M&Ms)
the narcissus, one-eyed, strains against
its makeshift chopstick stake to bloom. My pen,
leaking, blots and counts to ten, its indigo
dilation drawing water rings on the ceiling.

*

Ships' time, the East River's septet of islands,
each triangle mast raised to a tin star.
The wind settles. Scant block from the cold bank,
my love, bell-ringer at ten, at five, star-hive,
diminishes to a speck, the wind's fugue
tripling her internal rhyme. That watermark
white quartz I kept, Mab's stone, whose ripples
whet the air her horses reined, her rune her wand,
your eye for mine—your taloned verses held
small birds in air until they sang. When you
turned to speak I bit my tongue and thought
not mine. Come to me now. Heaven's geometry
is hesitation's proof; the triangle's sharp
note—tin hitting crystal—makes us stop.

*

The cranberry bogs—plush seats at La Fenice,
but the sky's aria after weeks of rain?
Bee sting, a swarm of buttercups, mercury
monogrammed with fever. Three wishes?
Even the simple know to ask for more—
the baby's hand a star, the blinded
measuring snake a Möbius strip. Who did Clotho
strangle but herself? Too many things
are possible in this world, Lachesis.
Fall is summer's bronze wing, it soars, then dips.
        Even Atropos is unpredictable—
a knife makes a fiddle of a breastbone,
a torn field mouse flicking rubies. My life
be my life, scarecrow punting at the moon.

Transit of mist, the blistered, peeling trees—
ice in the doorway makes us slip
and grab the brass knob that will and will not
turn. To choose a book is to choose—what?
Mrs. Dalloway, by the telephone,
steps out and shuts the door, the sky above Hyde Park
rickracked with clouds. Slight wind. Boot lifted above
a rainbow puddle. Do you remember?
We took a stick and twirled the gutter's oily
pond until the colors parted—Joseph's
coat, ragtag, the early sunset's bagatelle.
Love, if I could look at you—our life bleeds
into every corner; the sky's lavender lozenge
window, future tense, stores everything we do.

*

What rainbow amounts to anything?
The bracelet's lanyard on my wrist—woven
manacle, one a summer, *for mama*—
faint blush of mold on the sky's scud rim,
the horizon a bird blind high above Longnook
all bluff, the dune bowling down meteors,
its fatal hollows scored by falling timber,
spawn ghostwriting the low-tide mark.
Where are my happy loves? Right from wrong,
the simple past, asperity a rough
Venus, a mermaid and her twin seal
self, the blood red wax that stamps the letter
a welt on her fern tail, an x marking
              the spot where the light was.

Summer

FOR MAX RITVO

I

Three weeks until summer and then—what?
Midsummer's gravity makes our heads spin
each hour a gilt thread spool, winding through
the second hand, gossamer *fin de semaine,*
fin de siècle, fin slicing the water
of the too-cold-to-breathe bay, molten silver,
then receding as if we hadn't seen it,
sultan of *so long, see you tomorrow.*
      Dead man's fingers, lady slippers, a seal
who swims too close—too close for what? The needle
swerves. Our element chooses us. Water
fire, air, earth—the rosebush, Lazarus,
hot to the touch, gold reticulate, is love's
bull's-eye, attar rising from the rafters.

II

If I could make it stop I would. Was it
the crocodile Hook feared, or was it time?
The hour's arrow never misses, the gnomon,
glinting, cuts the Day-Glo sun to pieces.
In the ultraviolet palace of the Mermaid King
his girls wear scallop shells, one for each year
on their turquoise tails. Even they have birthdays,
why not you? Death, hold your ponies with one
hand, and stay awhile. On my desk, the lion's
paw lamp scavenged from the winter beach,
it's poppy-colored shells like the lit scales
of an enormous Trojan fish . . . teeth chattering,

its metronome time bomb *tsk tsk*—
when is giving up not giving in?

III   (CHILD'S POSE)

When Alice pulled the stopper, did she get
smaller, or did the world get larger? In
the bath, your nose bleeds a bouquet of tissue
roses, white stained red—adolescence
is to overdo it, but really? Thirty
stories up, our birds'-eye view is
the hummingbird tattoo on your bare head,
wings beating, too tiny and too big to see,
your wire-thin profile drawn upright, bones
        daring the air, marionette running on
the brain's dark marrow, tungsten for the fireflies'
freeze tag. Due south, the Chrysler Building's gauntlet
holds a lit syringe. We do and do not change.
Let me go from here to anywhere.

IV

That's it for now. And so we turn the page
your poems standing in for you, or—that's
not it, what's left of you, mediating
between what you'd call mind and body
and I, by now biting my lip, call grief,
        the lines netting the enormous air
like silver threads, the tails of Mr. Edward's
spiders with which they sail from ledge to branch
"as when the soul feels jarred by nervous thoughts
and catch on air." *Pace.* Your trousers worn
to mouse fur dragging on the stoop, your hip
prongs barely holding them aloft, the past

a phaeton, its sunlit reins bucking
at before and after, but there is no after.

v

Or is there? For once, when you rock back
on the chair I don't say *don't do that,*
forelegs lifting, hooves pawing the air—
Every departure's an elopement,
the shy cat fiddling while Rome sizzles,
spoon mirror flipping us upside down.
　　Son of Helios, rainbow fairy lights
blazing, when one light goes out they all
go out. At the top of the dune, the thorny
crowns of buried trees, their teeter-totter
branches a candelabra for the spiders'
silvery halo of threads. What a terrible
business it is, saying what you mean.
　　Speak, sky, the horizon scored by talons.

Anxiety

Cat claws on the heart's tin roof, each breath
a locomotive running off the rails,
the switching signal's warning rat-a-tat
I'm up too early, the alphabet net snags
and tears, moths, then motes, then gone. What I love,
I undo, eye for eye, tooth for tooth.
No one knows me, matchstick Guy Fawkes doll,
my burnt head micro-ember sunset gleams,
day moon hostage to the dark's slant dream.
What ghosts I have I won't or can't give up.
Impossible to love or leave, poor self
banging its head, wanting—what?
As if I knew what I meant or wanted,
baby voice humming: mouth skull smile.

The Impulse Wants Company

FOR TROY SCHUMACHER AND ELLIS LUDWIG-LEONE

I

Funnel of trees, bees, corkscrew
　　pines, the sky a map with a gold badge,

less wind where the grass is bent
　　but the waves a white hedge—

　　　　　fanfare-breaking, curling under. Torque.
Froth. When we were children we came
　　to the beach every day and ran

　　　　　down the high dune
to the water.
　　　　I was a water nymph
there was a hole in the bucket
　　　we ran—

　　　somersault—

II

Seesaw. The green world
white and blue, salt-stripped—
　　too big, sky too far, the sweet air

　　　—bright cartwheel the dune rolling over itself
　　　　　hurry—the sandpiper
　　　　　leaves a snakeprint
　　　　　　in the sharp sand

. . .

    our scales shine in the wet sun
                flipping
                        —a quick dolphin

its flank silver slicing the water
                pulling the swimmer
into the blue distance like a gaze.

The wind cocks its ear—

        a steady hum, the gills
                of the day opening

and shutting, sheen reflection
                a dream of summer

        —toe in the water—

umbrella a sunflower,
your body unfolding

                —blade-bone
                        wrist hip

            the sand turning
                its toes under,

            the sun a pinhole
camera. Shadow.

III

                  The letters swim—*You said*
that wasn't it—

   I meant—

it's too hot to fight too bright.
   Have you been in? Are you going

      in? Come on! Oh leave me
be—You're the water rat,

you're the spoilsport,
   Watcha looking at?

Seahorse, minnow, crab claw,
   Neptune a phoenix, horsing
around—*All winter I dreamed*
  of the beach

     and here we are
lizards—when I think—

a walk? *On this beach*

the girl I was lengthening
   and shortening her shadow
      hammered to silver—

   a shape in the sand far out.
      I see a boat, a cloud, they are
        waving from the boat—

. . .

He never goes in. *Why
is it such a big deal?*
The impulse wants
company.

Out in the water the whales
sing their beautiful warnings
blue fire lit in water, the sand

infinitesimally sinking as the water

rises, the earth itself the selkie
half-human, in love
with herself who returns

IV

to the sea, quaking, salt stars
on her skin, each one
a Catherine wheel, pirouette,

a tiny galaxy, its
Möbius strip
giving the selkie back—
slick
dangerous—to herself

and others. *She'll be the death of me.*
But he puts on her spangled cloak
and drifts out or actually

. . .

paddles, selvage between air
     and water indistinguishable
      —hair, feather, scale, fin—

until he is smaller then gone but
  gigantic, the waves and
     the sea cradling him until he

lets go, cells sequins
  sloughing off, distilled
   swallowed

by the sea which is a whale
    made of sky.

   The dream which is
      dry land inside out

swallowed

so that the scene on the beach—
  telling the story of
    a disappearance, a frisson,

v

life opening to swallow someone

 who gave no sign

really, it can happen anytime
  with so little provocation,
   disaster, the stars

. . .

misaligned, or set straight
in a way that was impossible to
        imagine, standing as we do

with our hands shielding our eyes
        to block the sun,
            is it the beach

which is drowning, the lover
        who wants to get away
                drowned by leaving

alchemical,
        regretting
                what was always

going to happen, a crescendo
        which is only natural
                when we think about loss—or

                    what passes for it
leaving the others—terrestrial
        incapable of leaving, then gone—

(CODA)

The dream of an ending
        the reluctant swimmer returning—

. . .

in a space carved from shadow and air
    dusk phosphorescent, a moonshell

fish, dolphin, minnow bird-bright blue—

Shark

The Muse of History

I   CLIO

let my tongue cleave to the roof of my mouth

     The past's fantasia cannot hold or let
us go. Flycatcher catching itself in
the pool's glint gaze, Samarkand where Tamerlane
hewed his bloody thread, unspooling across
the hacked-to-pieces field, a triple axle
splitting Clio's cataract, muddy then
clear, the opal of a rain-sheened open
eye that looks at nothing but yet holds
our look.
               Euterpe, my head is in my hands.
Flies speckle the field. The sizer, hissing,
straps dynamite to a waist no bigger
than a fly's wingspan, but the daughters
of Babylon do not tarry—the road flares
burn blue, bog irises, erect, quivering.

II   CHARLESTON

How shall we sing the Lord's song in a strange land?

The coiled snake sheds and eats itself, its bitten
tail an omphalos, the arrowhead's
stung fire hitting the scorched bull's-eye,
the crooning singer stopped mid-note, his silent
measure hung in air, a pillow slip, cotton

turning to cloud, immeasurable—
the President, singing.
                At Appomattox,
when General Lee said to Ely S. Parker,
a Senecan, who recorded the terms
of the surrender, "It is good to have
a real American here," he replied, "Sir,
we are all Americans." The century
folds, a white flag rent with frazzled tears.
Let my demons rage so I know who they are.

III   THE GONE WORLD

   O daughter of Babylon

The calico licks each knuckle to a moonscape,
her velvet pupils two quotation marks.
        What's the opposite of oxygen?
Pure carbonation, the children trail their cartoon
balloons past where last night, sleepless on
my duck blind–barge, I steered the ragged sofa
across Persia's raveled coast and ran aground.
Cat and fiddle, dish and spoon, their voices
tinsel, threading time's slit-eye needle—
Does the moon hold water? The moon, or our
idea of it? Shall I come kiss you? *Yes, please.*
Fugitive, the cut-throat sparrow captive
bangs its head and takes the future's measure,
an echo climbing Eurydice's stair.

IV AT HOME

we hanged our harps upon the willows

Every moment's a time bomb. The scorpion
inside a cage of flame will strike himself,
two of them will kill each other, black
carapace glimpsed through the needle's eye.
The flame darting where you laid it down
is Giotto's circle lit with paraffin,
your halo full of whirring bees. Come, lost
one, out of the shadows—the children's
sparklers constellate the sequined lawn,
Orion's arrows pinning fallen stars.
No man meets me. I strut the stair, half-dare
myself to miss the tread, shy spider,
all hands and legs—*If you don't see me,*
you ain't gonna have to wonder why.

V INSIDE OUT

If I forget thee, O Jerusalem

FOR MICHAEL VINCENT MILLER

Say what you see. I see a door. *A door?*
Is it open or closed? It is opening.
No, it's closing. Now it's closed, I think.
I think it's closed. *Where is the door? What*
sort of door is it? An inside door,
the door of a room. *Which room?* When
I was a child. A slipper of light.
But it's the wrong door! *Is there another door?*
When Charlemagne invited Alcuin
of York to Aachen to supervise the new

clear handwriting of God, the herded letters
jumped the fence like lambs. Moss on the door,
the hinges rusted shut, damp green on green.
I put my ear to it, the thick plank vibrating.

The Fogbow

FOR ADRIEN AMZALLAG

A day of offshore weather, the wet cove
overhung with elms, the sun cocooned
in cloud, the waves scrolling under and over.
We talked among ourselves. You read *Tartuffe*.
"In winter," you said, "in Frankfurt when I can't sleep,
I think of this sound." Heavy, foam-flecked,
two sleek-headed seals, their whiskers broom bristles,
bobbed not ten feet away. Your finger checked
the damp page of your book. When we next looked,
not a rainbow but a fogbow over the water—
a silver pencil line inside the sky's margins,
a circumflex that marked the barely there
that quickened us as if we'd seen a ghost
in the picture the fog had drawn in air.

Japanese Poems

Between the bent boughs
of the splayed sumac, the silver
owl rests his head.

The perimeter
left by your absence is long
to walk in one day.

The angel in her
credenza of extreme beauty
dogs swim the river.

I look for my heart
by the lamp where the light is
skitter in the wet black leaves.

Blue Vase

Because you like to sleep with curtains drawn,
    at dawn I rose and pulled the velvet tight.

You stirred, then set your hand back on my hip,
    the bed a ship in sleep's doubled plunging

wave on wave, until as though a lighthouse
    beam had crossed the room: the vase between

the windows suddenly ablaze, a spirit,
    seized, inside its amethyst blue gaze.

What's that? you said. A slip of light, untamed,
    had turned the vase into a crystal ball,

whose blue eye looked back at us, amazed, two
    sleepers startled in each other's arms,

while day lapped at night's extinguished edge,
    adrift between the past and future tense,

    a blue moon for an instant caught in its chipped
        sapphire—love enduring, give or take.

Sunday

I   EARLY MORNING

The rain, gray god with its huge hands
has shredded the roses, and clapping
kept us up all night, the bridge washed out,
the troll waiting to gobble a goat.
How long has he been there, wet and cold,
             impatient, starving, his coat
rent with welts and matted with mist?

             Father, thundering, his voice full
of bracken and leaves, leaves that in
the autumn clogged the gutters. *Who*
goes over the bridge? Who goes there?
      the billy goats stammering, pawing
the air. But I am the goat and the troll,
and so cannot pass nor grant passage.

II

The high meadow filled with sweet grass!
The spindle puts the moon to bed,
the window latched, the sheets pulled tight,
pincushion star, ram butting his head,
my brother and sister behind and ahead—
his sister was no use to him either,
                  she took what was his, cat's cradle

bridge made of sharp goats' thread. Who
goes there now, over the rickety
bridge? Tiny steps, lickety-split,

my place is in the pause between
          the thunder and the bridge; Father
shouting over the torn white water.
hoofprints mark the place last seen.

III   AT THE MUSEUM (BELLOWS)

FOR ALEXANDER NEMEROV

     The man in the left hand corner
of Bellows's picture of the Dempsey-Firpo
fight, the picture a dream, so not a real
fight—a picture of a fight—his flayed hide
just visible under his blue pinstripes,
the watcher and the fighter
          indistinguishable, one inside

the other, lion and lion tamer,
the paint daubs faces or fingerprints
and the lights staring and staring across
          the fretwork of the ring, and Bellows
himself, next to him, looking surprised,
as if to be there was to give himself up
without our noticing it, as we all do

in a gesture, or word, leaving something
behind we should have taken with us
          or even guarded, a way of not letting
something be over and done with.
The fight was over in four minutes flat.
A curious thing about the painting
is that Bellows chose to show us

. . .

the moment when Firpo sent Dempsey
careening, with a blow to the jaw,
one of the two times he laid him out,
and we, with the spectators crammed
            into the foreground of the picture,
have to help push Dempsey back
into the ring where two-and-a-half

minutes later he will defeat Firpo,
who went down four times to his two.
In Assisi, at the Basilica di San Francesco,
            in the panel in which Giotto depicts
the moment Francis gives away
his worldly goods, the palm that Francis
raises up to the hand that is reaching

down to him from heaven, a hand out
of the blue, open, ready to give or
receive wonders, is the same hand
in Bellows's picture raised behind Dempsey—
            one wing of a dove, the impulse is
to press our own palms to it, and despite
our better judgment, to hurl him back.

IV   BLACKBIRDS

A song that Father liked to sing:
      a dozen blackbirds baked alive
but still alive when they did bring
      the pie to set before the king—
what a flurry when the pie was cut!
      The birds cawed madly as they rose—

blackbirds flapping blackened wings
 who circled back to snip your nose!

 I see the moon, the moon sees me,
shining on the apple tree . . .
 don't sit under the apple tree
with anyone else but me—
 no, no, with anyone else but me . . .
sound of hurry, over the bridge.

V   AT THE MUSEUM (WYETH)

 As always, we want something from the dead,
even the blackbird, stiff in a kind of grassy net,
 its black leather gangster feet curled up
as if holding on to something it let go—
 and beyond, to the right, inevitably, a house—
black-shuttered with its high grey wing,

 its bones buried deep in the earth like a beast
which once took flight, bones with the imprint
 of feathers, that print repeated in the faraway trees
on a rise to the left of the house, a good distance
 away, as if the trees had been painted by pressing
a painted leaf to the canvas, the spine

 the tablature of a feather, or fish, the scales
clearly marked in miniature, although we know
 the trees are much bigger than the blackbird
so stock-still in the spiky grass, so lately landed,
 its glossy mourning coat spit-shined. Under
those trees, a short distance from the house

. . .

    as nowhere else in the picture, a moment
of repose, the sun on the warm bark, the circle
    of cool beneath. But the bird holds us fast,
a shadow cast by moonlight, the flowers
        beside it articulate as the delphiniums
in *La Primavera,* at the Uffizi, at which we

        paused until we could look no longer at
an extreme propensity for beauty, as though it
        might explode in smithereens. Autumn,
the seedpods are moth-eaten moons, dry, rattling.
        In Wyeth's more famous picture, the girl
stranded in the foreground in a clutch of weeds

        her awkward limbs stretching in the hissing grass
is in the same place in the picture plane
        as the blackbird, we all agreed with this,
the woman in the white hat—why a hat,
        inside the museum, and her friend, smaller,
dressed all in black, black shoes, black stockings,

        black dress, although it is summer.
At once we want to help her as she reaches
the unbridgeable distance of the field
        and the meadow filled with rough grass
although it's not so evident how to help her
        for even now our heavy limbs twitch with

enchantment, caught by a dream in which
        it is impossible to move except by slithering.
In my sleep you said I said—*too many people.*
        The black house is a ship on the horizon,

every light on, or the moon that looks
      as if it is following us but from which

we are always veering away, the white wolf
      snapping at our heels, goading us to cross
the bridge or waiting for us by the water
      its white face wavering under the pilings.
The girl is a blackbird in the high grass;
      it is natural to mistake one for the other

when it is so difficult despite the painter's
efforts, herculean, really, to see clearly—

VI   SATURDAY NIGHT (AT THE BALLET)

    Puck, above a game of flashlight tag
the tiniest fairy pirouetting like a dervish—
the honeysuckle wood alit, one pointed
green-shod foot dangling, like the hand that reached
down to Francis to pull him up to heaven
or rebuke him, or the white hand coming
out of the darkness over the ring: counting
one, two, three, alley, alley, innisfree—
the three goats balking at the bridge, Father
bellowing over the rushing water
the river loud, rearing its head, foam rushing past
its eyes and ears, Father clamoring, needing
something—the moment we know
      it has come to nothing.

VII   (THE DREAM)

The heavens shift.
And presto! the tilted abacus
of stars slides back in place, twilight's worn edge rubbed
to a sheen. Queen, ass, Indian child, love-lit quartet, slipping
   as the constellations do
               behind Gaia's unearthly tilt
leaving us in night's cooler, less demanding air
               where our taxi driver has his phone
on speaker: twenty minutes of harangue,
   a hornet trapped inside a troika, the driver
               silent except once to say,
interrupting the ceaseless string of epithets,

      "You are the woman of my dreams."
   The avenue slick before the curb,
lights turn from red to green. Remember? The crescent
moon scar on my knee—

      Rain patters the windshield, the lights
from the bodega spatter lime and pink.
   A folded scene.
         Above, the moon—
   another night before a halt.

VIII   EVENING AND MORNING

Morning lit by evening's lantern, the cat
a baby falling from the broken bough,
childhood's terrible litter of fear.
I am the goat and the goat is me. I see the moon,
the moon sees me. And if I die before I wake,
the spirit leaving the body as we sleep
as Giacomo said in the gospel—who said it, where?

if the spirit leaves my body where does it go?
—and in the dark the pine knots watching
and your eyes big in the dark, and the sound of breathing.
In your sleep you said *too many people.*
I woke you in the dark and I took you by the hand—
How far is the moon? If I folded this piece of paper?
But then you would never get there, remember?
And your total disregard of me—
Twilight's rainbow a lasso fetching the moon from the water.
When I was walking I fell from the curb.
You did not. *I did, I did.*

IX   THE COVE

The three children not far off
cross the road to the water
and into the hot high grass,
their feet light on the flattened
stalks of the cattails that line
the swale like pale raffia
woven expressly for that

purpose, as if the landscape
was a diorama made
of glassine, straw, and folded
paper. Whose children are they—
one, two, three, walking to
the ruined, silvery, splintery
boat, that looks like a whale come

ashore in the pocket cove
which opens at high tide like
a giantess's compact?

There is another smaller
shadow, pulling a kite—or
no, a pull-toy dog, which barks
at an upturned horseshoe crab

and a stained, eyeless, gray-brown
gull. How oddly sound travels
over water. Underfoot
the sun-crazed hermit crabs run
helter-skelter to their bomb
shelters under the wet sand,
where at dead low tide the marsh

makes a kind of long humped bridge
of itself to the rapt cove
and the ruined quiet. *Psst* says
the wind. The children run at
it, lowing their heads, making
horns with their fingers, bashing
themselves in it and through it.

X   CASE SENSITIVE

Two days I've forgotten where I'm going,
New York's crossword up and down a litter
of numbers and letters. I spin on the grid,
round hole in a square peg, each step a rope
bridge hung in air, my tongue a troll who eats
my words, my goat-fur cloak held fast by Psyche's
brooch. "Smile, liebling, you have your whole life
ahead of you." *Hold on tight.* Even the dead
won't speak to me, my sharp hooves beating
the bank's slick grass, the bog oak's muddy rune.

Bee disheveled on the stairs, the storm
rattling the panes. *"I dreamed I walked and walked
and could not find my way."* Dear God, let me
keep my dreams to myself and do no harm.

Dear and Blackbirds

e tu allor li priega
per quello amor che i mena, ed ei verranno
—DANTE, *INFERNO*, CANTO V

One by one they walk down
the fence of trees by the swimming pool,
    delicate endearments, their hooves

just printing the dew-drenched lawn
with arrowheads. From the long table
    where months ago we ate

breakfast, they are just visible,
the small things we say to each other—
    ti penso e ti bacio

written in the cold grass, that if we were
barefoot would pierce our feet.
        The other morning, early,

on Broadway, when you must admit
it was a miracle we were still
        standing—we were rushing

there was no time for anything—you said
"this weather is perfect" and raised
        your shirt to let the faint chill

touch your skin, and I grazed
my hand over it, feeding like a blackbird,
    un corvo, un uccello nero,

a raven, which can be one who
is ravenous, the word, translated, *caro,*
        windblown for once into flesh.

Your Mother Dancing on the Table

(FIESOLE 1966)

     In the long low living room
after everyone has gone,
your mother in a sleeveless
shift dress made out of some stiff
     turquoise material
is dancing on the table.

     It's a cold night. She is
not wearing stockings. She has
kicked off her shoes. In her bare
feet, long arms aloft, she is
     conducting Mozart, which
streams from the turntable

     to the stereo speakers,
then eddies, waves lapping the
huge untidy room, where she
is just now beautifully
     alone for one minute.
Upstairs you and your sister

     are asleep. Your grandmother
is reading in the next room.
It is the year the Arno
flooded. Your grandmother's own
     house is underwater.
Her bookmark is embossed with

     a crescent moon C, her own
watermark. Her earrings are
diamond clips. Her feet are dry.

Her neighbors were rescued from
            their roofs and pulled from their
windows. What's that noise? you asked

            your sister. She is six, she
is two years older, she can
read; in her white nightgown she
is a dandelion. You
            are not asleep—really, it
is early evening, not night

            at all. You are playing a
game with counters, she has the
shoe and you have the hat, and
you run down the hall to fetch
            your grandmother, who puts
down her open book and in

            stocking feet walks downstairs with
you and your sister. The word
you use when you tell me this
story is *accomplices,*
            in the language that first
belonged to your mother and

            now we use between us. In
the living room at the foot
of the stairs your mother was
still dancing, her body a
            tuning fork, conducting
the music. Stop it! your sister

    cried out, and tried to shield you
so you would not see. "Don't be
so puritanical," said

your mother, a word that your
		sister did not know but
in the language in which your

		mother spoke to her, she heard
a word she both did and did not
not know, a bad thing, and she
began to hit your mother on
		the legs, to make her come
down from the table, as the

		tide of sound roared under her.
Outrageous! your grandmother
said—she'd always known about
your mother and here was proof!
		Your black hair was damp from
your bath. Your light blue cotton

		pajamas were buttoned to
the neck. Your body was sleek
as a badger's, a body
to which nothing much had yet
		happened, the secret life
of the body that occurs,

		to us and in us in small
increments, fiercely, subtly,
as it did the afternoon
you told me this story—but
		even then you knew you
had never seen anything

		more beautiful than the sight
of your mother dancing on
the table, Mozart coursing

under her above
              the flooded city, through
the open shutters into

              the green twilight, as when the
angel said to Tobias:
see the fish flashing in the
river. Half a century
      later, six stories up,
blocks from the Hudson, you say

              to me, I missed you, I had
music on before people
came and I was dancing. Now
you ask me to listen to
              you and I do, and what
I hear is the sound of your

              mother's bare feet keeping time
as she danced on the table,
the high notes her hands, quick stars
in quickened air, the music—
              the moment before she
                            stopped and after it.

From Metaphysicks

METAPHYSICK FOR THE NEW YEAR

If Love would have her way with us
      she'd bind us lip to brow and brow
to knee, and wind a lariat
         of leaves about Love's moment that
in it holds all time. But you
        and I are sick of love. The year
has turned. My heart, where nothing sat—
      a wreath Love bound, that by our will
        will prove a collar or a crown.

MID-JANUARY

  "Indeed it is the first day again and again of everything."

In deed each day is made anew—
      Time's gaze in time turns trespass true;
Love's tempered arrows hit and miss
        and hit their mark, and prick out words
    the blind by touch can read. For when
      birds touch down upon a pond's blue
      eye, by concentric rings its iris
widens. Time, sit by Love's side.
      The night unfolds tomorrow's news.

A GAME OF CHESS

A board atilt between two chairs.
      How long, Love asks, has this gone on?
In dream patois will mimics whim—
    the Queen remits her bracelets, viziers,
      wits, and pawns her heart to colonize
the King, who retreating draws in air
      a triad now become a square.
On which he sits. Radiant, Love
      pulls that throne from under him.

ANATOMY

If you court heartbreak you may marry
    it. Love balks, protests, grieves, tarries—
      The long way round a slipknot noose,
    no hanging, but had a heart ankle,
      wrist, knee (for though it be a living
        thing it does not walk, live, coo)—
Wrong. These many limbs in traction.
    For the heart do sup, cry, sleep, rankle.

CATHEXIS

If I could take my heart by stealth
and place it in my heel, so that
    my ribs might make a belfry where
      love's bell might forge anew a tongue—

and then by walking so repair
        the newborn changeling to brute health
I'd whistle as I walked the route—
      or that's the tale I tell myself.

CODA

Folly, to think rhyme could make stand
that at which Love throws up its hands.

Conversazione

Codesto solo oggi possiamo dirti,
ciò che non *siamo, ciò che* non *vogliamo.*
—MONTALE

A small breath lifting the curtain,
   here, not here, now tell me which—
      and in the avenue Pasternak's

      snowflakes, white moths circling
      the Hudson's streetlamps, like my body
astral, touching yours in transit,

a bride's ghost veil, a white egret
   under a waterfall, and
      from a palazzo of clouds, a boy

      falling into your arms—
a trumpet's adagio, and the
sound you make clearing your throat, a latch

opening, and I slipped through it
   alone though I did not know
      it then, the sound magnetized, the split

      song heard by a dog who
   would later be fed glass, cuttlefish
bones fed to the birds. I ate from

the hand I have made you almost
   wholly without your consent,
      and you walked to the river without

      me, warming my hands by
   blowing on them, the ceiling fan a
starburst shredding the air, the bed

. . .

Agostino's boat, octopus
　　　pots on the wharf, the bleached sheets
　　　　　puckering. *Don't you know I like storms?*

　　　　　Fifty blocks north, the snow,
　　　lace on the stoop, is sand blown in from
the desert where the red cow lows

and cries for her calf. *Mi manchi*
　　　perche non sei qui, these lines
　　　　　between tenses, one eye winked shut, far.

Late Afternoon

FOR ALICE TRUAX

Three pairs of binoculars but which one works—
why do we say "pair" when we mean one?
What we see is what we are—the swimming
pool's black shadow eye-mote, a mole, drowned,
its stiff bird feet a blurred ideogram.
Fetch the net. The day's stuck fast. Feverish
July, lilies mark the lawn, crimson
yellow, tangerine—a Palio, each bloom
a pony with its tongue mete out. Beyond
the big white tent, a giant's handkerchief,
the red-hot smokehouse writes its blue cursive.
When I was a girl, I made friends with a willow
and gave it the gift of my loneliness—
How near is near? How far is far?

Class Picture

I'm the eighth tallest. How do you know?
For the class picture, we stood in line.
When we were smaller I came third but now—
Dreaming my way that night back forty years
I saw, or thought I saw myself, one girl
in a staggered row of girls, tiers reaching up
astride a hill or bandstand, head turned
to speak into the ear of the next girl.
I felt my too hot shirt, my hank of hair,
my purposely averted gaze; I had
no friend but being not there, unrecorded
except by a gigantic eye, looking
down from a great mesmerizing height . . .
though I could not have said that then, or why.

Rainy Day Fugue

The rain on the roof splits
into drops, one, then another,
a splatter of opals, and then
pools on the window ledge
where someone—when
was it?—left the mark
of a hammer set down
before the paint dried
to worn blue, the color
of the sky before it's fully
light, when it isn't raining.

Beneath the rain the quiet
is tremendous, hollowing out
the day that expands endlessly
one followed by another
and a third, indistinguishable,
from one another, a set
of moving mirrored shadows.
A diving bell from which, today,
it feels—unlikely—to emerge.
Outside, the rain sluices
down the bent azaleas,

pooling in the declivities
of the sharp flagstones
and the mossy spaces
between them. The rain comes
from far away, it is almost
impossible to imagine it,
the acres of cloud bound
over this part of the earth,

but even so a drop lands.
A blue diamond squirreled
in the cup of a leaf curling

on the parapet, a leaf from
the desiccated geranium.
Beneath the umbrella of the roof,
silence. The words of the book
swim, minnows in a stream
strung with gilt lozenges
from the reading light—
which clear only to wobble
again. What is it made of,
the lump in the throat—
feathers, or coal? Neither.

Or has the rain come,
somehow, inside?
It is tears. And the bird
outside the window who
seems not to know it is
raining, or for its own reasons
is pretending not to know,
sings one note, then another.
Or is it two birds, talking
together? The rain
knits itself on the long needles

of latitude and longitude
along the bridges and avenues
where the sodden leaves
make tracks of brown and gold
across the tarmac and clog
the gutters, the water rising
until the house, the walls,
the curtains printed with

rickshaws and flowers, your
sweater, are made of mist.
    Once years ago

I was riding a bicycle
on the hill and the blue
reared up at the bent arm
of the road and I thought
mountain, or *cloud.* It was
the sea, blue and gigantic,
a V of paint at the notch
of the turning. A friend
told me the other day
that for the tightrope walker
the most treacherous
moment is the turning,

reaching a destination
only to turn back the way
he came. The rain
keeps its colloquy
on the roof. When it pauses
the birds make a tremendous
noise, beating their wings
as if to dry them, tracing
arcs in the damp air, as
if they had been waiting
keenly for this one moment

in which to make themselves
heard, white on white on
white, their beaks scribbling
and in the mind's cool
barely open eye the sky turns
itself inside out, seamlessly
reflected in water.

Or as the page does now
where beyond its wrought
iron fences, pools and hills

rise in a rain-soaked landscape,
both near and far, birds,
and what look like birds,
and small houses, their roofs
glistening, and the trees
heavy with water,
which we would see
if only once more we
could manage it—on
the page which for
this hour hasn't turned.

II

A story. Summer. I remember
bees in the clover, the vivid nasturtiums
climbing the speckled foxgloves, the smell
of shells lining the path, rot and seawater.
Wasps thrummed in the pine hollow,
the sun was so hot it could burn
a hole in paper if you put a glass to it.

       Inside the doorknobs
were too hot to touch.
The air was still. The birds I recall
were finches and wrens, you knew
the names of birds and I knew the names
of flowers. It was enough to go on.

This is a wrong turn. Start again.

A story. It is summer. Bees
in the clover. And I—what
was I doing, on the green hill?
Reading. I was reading
or pretending to read—
it is hard to tell at this
distance. Or to say what
I was feeling, though still
even now I see the birches
and hear the voice of the owl.
Tread lightly here. A hiss
in the grass. The mill
wheel turning the sleeve
of the sky. The other day
—it is thirty years later—
I came upon that paragraph
I was pretending to read
    that day on the hillside
the light strong through
the birches, the words—
the words darting.

    But she begged him to let
her alone, she almost pushed
him back; she drew Verena out
    into the dark freshness, closing
the door of the house behind her. There
was a splendid sky, all blue-black
    and silver—a sparkling wintry
vault, where the stars were like
    a myriad points of ice.

The letters worn, where my eyes
had grazed them.

III

What says the brown wren?
Be better off dead.
What says the jackanapes—
stand on your head.
What says the violet?
What says the hen?
If you don't love me
caulk the bucket, dull the blade,
forget left luggage
left unclaimed
cat in the bag, cow in the barn,
quiet the bells,
what made you think
you could do me harm?

She'll die of hunger
say the geese in the pond.
A crown of beetles round her head,
Saucy puts herself to bed.
Star in the manger
hang it by the door—
if you come calling
I won't be there anymore.
Pinto pony gallops
by the ragged track
at a zebra crossing
you need to look both ways.
If you come back to me,
if you can find your way

the cat will say good morning
and open up the door.
The Appaloosa's hide
speckled brown and grey—

is it how he sees it,
that it got that way?
My head is in the oven
my heart has ruled my head
when you see me coming
I'll head straight away.
One hen lays white eggs,
and Araucana blue—
which one do you think
breaks my heart in two?

IV

The rain on the roof
ice in the eaves
and between, the up
and down lines, straight
and round, a tunnel
strung sideways. If
I put up my hands
the ivy strays, long
sentences, telling
stories. The rain
on the roof flushes
cold tears. Only
one bird, that I hear.
What does it say?
How long must I stay?

NEXT DAY

New Poems

Marina

The sky's grey mantle over me
    sewn with lapis lazuli—
        the terrible sky, where you walk
in our city not thinking of me—

Your indifference bedecks me—
        the locomotive
of my heart rattles past the crepe myrtle,
the leaves startled, buds like jewels.

The sun has no business in the sky
    nor does the moon, nor the myrtle
or its spattered blooms, nor your gaze

now that you have turned from me.
    I am gauze printed by twilight, barely a body—

After Anna Akhmatova

As the future ripens in the past, . . .
a terrible festival of dead leaves

The trees talk quietly among themselves
the thrush sings its brown song brushed with blue
the roses from the bodega open in the vase—
and under the streetlight the long shadows

tarnishing the day as we know it—if I ask for
a stone you give me a stone, if I ask for water
I do not get water, everything I love weighed
and found wanting, as if the world knew how

to give answers to questions. In the long
generous shadow of history, I wake and wonder
how long it can go on, my ear touching
your lips, asking, what are you thinking—

while in the capital the lion stalks his cage,
and on the veld the scorched banyans bend
under their fruit, the camps charred, no one
to pick it. A long time ago, after months

when death came so quickly to us it was
as if we had written an invitation, crows
settled in the ghost trees. There is my
mother, you said, and my father. It goes on.

April

Now out of this vast silence
the cherry trees scraping their gnarled limbs
    on the sky, and the wind hurls down
a flurry of petals, a snowstorm really

a thousand prints on the wet pavement,
each one a pair of white shutters, opening.

Numinous, the souls of the dead, and now you
. . . among them— an intake of breath.

How little it seems to me now,
we knew each other.

But still, it is so beautiful, the place where you were—
    a table, two chairs, a tree growing up
right through the floor, and outside,

a flicker of swallows in the hedgerows,
      the tulips' purple chevrons a row of arrowheads.

. . . It is wherever you
want to be, although by now you are
beyond wanting. Or at least that's
    what they say of the dead.

The place where you were holds the light
the way the leaves do after dusk
when small animals conduct

their assignations—the shrew, the mouse, the mole
running their etudes in the mossy shadows.

. . . You were always so
afraid of falling short. If only you hadn't
done such a good job of dying.

But it is so
beautiful where you were, above
the garden, where it is snowing, this morning in April,
    on the bleached white pansies,

the downed cherry blossoms
. . .
where you so often sat,
        talking and talking.

Athena

As you imagined me, I came
    to you, near as the sound of an owl
        in the clearing, then nearer,

my eyes two moons, one holding
    the gaze of another, silver
        under an olive leaf—bridle,

bit, chariot, ship, the water chinning
    the scant prow, shearwater
        splitting the gold waves.

Spirit-bubble, I held your own beam
    level and then squared, a kite
        that dove among the islands,

chasing its own tail of light that
    left only its leavings, as autumn
        scatters summer when it

arrives. Near to the shore, linen
    beat to my breath on the bank,
        near to the fields, wool

caught on the brambles where
    the sheep ate from my hand
        but you drew back! Then

I knew to draw nearer, and nearer
    still—and draw, us two together
        on the table's compass flower

a lure pulled through the storm's
        pale eye like a thread that reins
            a needle's stride, the weft

disguised, a beggar's lifeline crossed
        by a silver track, a snail's reversing
            journey back, the sails

laundry on a broomstick mast
        that like a weathercock veers
            until it meets fair weather:

your near hand, held fast
        in mine. You, beloved,
            though not I, grow old.

Clytemnestra

Sky streaked with azure and bloodred.
    No wind.
No oar.

That memory swift-hooved, tramples itself,
    the cart wheel rutting in the ditch
        as if the spokes

would turn backward. That sound
    racks my sleep.
        Quiet now.

And I took my own dove
    in bridal raiment to meet Achilles.
    And you.

—No wind.
    No oar.
        A mouse-tail mattered less to me

a withered leaf
    that borne
        on a fast wind

becomes a boat, a furrow
    in the wild water—
        a breath

then sinks.
    Less than that, that took
        my love, my thrush

　　　　　　my heart forfeit.

　　　　　　And you, it was you
　　　took her from me!

No god cares where I lay my head

I don't care where I make my bed

My bond unmade where my sweet deer lies.

Italian Lesson

FOR SIMONA LORENZINI

the boy plays with the horse   il ragazzo gioca con il cavallo
the seasons change   le stagioni cambiano
I have never seen a volcano   non ho mai visto un vulcano
we need wood for the fire   abbiamo bisogno di legno per il fuoco
the wet wood is not good   il legno bagnato non è buono
he saw smoke in the sky   ha visto fumo nel cielo
then it is a volcano   allora è un vulcano
there is sand in my shoes   c'è sabbia nelle mie scarpe
the children build castles   i bambini costruiscono i castelli
the clouds were getting darker   le nuvole stanno diventando più scure
we could see nothing but fog   non vedevamo niente a parte la nebbia
the fog is a cloud on the ground   la nebbia è una nuvola sul pavimento
the fog doesn't let us see anything   la nebbia non ci lasciava vedere nulla
there is a flower on the bed   c'è un fiore sul letto
there is a flower on the table   c'è un fiore sul tavolo
we are in the forest   siamo nella foresta
it is dangerous to swim in the lake   è pericoloso nuotare nel lago
I have only a small garden   ho solo un piccolo giardino
we can hear the ocean from here   possiamo sentire l'oceano da qua
where do you see the moon?   dove vedi la luna?
she sees the sea   lei vede il mare
the mountain climate is different   il clima di montagna è diverso
it could rain this evening   potrebbe piovere stasera
the rain follows me everywhere   la pioggia mi segue dappertutto
he sees the sky   lui vede il cielo
the region has many rivers   la regione ha molti fiumi
are you lost? heaven is far from here   ti sei perso? il cielo è lontano da
                                                                                    qua
which planet are you on?   su quale pianeta ti trovi?
the sea is not blue today   il mare non è azzurro oggi
the storm has passed   il temporale è passato
in autumn the moon is beautiful   in autunno la luna è bella

the snake waits under the rock   il serpente aspetta sotto la roccia

the children play in the snow in December   i bambini giocano nella
neve a dicembre

the snow is beautiful   la neve è bellissima

this morning we go to look at the sunrise   questa mattina andiamo a
guardare l'alba

there wasn't a cloud in the sky   non c'era una nuvola nel cielo

the sea, the hills, the little mountains   il mare, le colline, e le piccole
montagne

yesterday I went fishing in the river   ieri sono andato a pescare nel
fiume

the sun this evening is not yellow it is orange   il sole stasera non è giallo
è arancione

how many stars do you see?   quante stelle vedi?

there are many stars in the universe   ci sono molte stelle nell'universo

At Putney

Pink scud clouds over the bridges,
    Vauxhall, Lambeth, Battersea,

spider-work. Black. The syllables
    of water, black. *Go. Stay.* Met

in air, met in water and I a child
    of summer born far from here

on a Thursday. A Thursday, you say?
    Far to go and full of woe.

And what year was it, the house
    a page torn from the calendar,

a foolscap boat filled with paper
    ballast, bisecting the waves

until they parted, impossible to let
    a single page go, and the thud

when the tide hit the bank? A year
    to remember. Give me your hand

across the water. Once I went down
    when the tide was out and the stones

ashimmer, obsidian in the moonlight,
    the ivy brackish and the toads

dry in their den. Come out
    from the fountain, maenad

made of green stone, moss-flecked
bone and your teeth chattering.

The Lost Hour (Eastern Standard Time)

building diminutive boats
. . . for sailing beyond the borderline of time.
—CZESŁAW MIŁOSZ

I

Rain on the skylight \
   on the black window
soft hiss, what might have been said

    —resist saying now what it might
      have been, or said—

the rain knows
    it wouldn't make any difference
      have made a difference,

the lost hour a sodden
    stray cat

    —was that her,
is it?—

un'ombra nel'angolo,

    jackdaws asleep in their wet stick
        nests.

Upstairs, the clocks let it go,
downstairs,
   the clocks
      let it go,

  —

they know what's what,
time to give up the ghost

—but what is it supposed
   to do with itself, gone, bereft,

                pushing its wheelbarrow full of tears, was it?—

it's time

   but this one won't, violet pie-face
      stubborn, blinking, awake
                    hoop rolling
         down a long muddy hill

a track in the sward

teetering but upright
      taking
         the corner

   —the wheelbarrow, now just stop it
      whatever do you want all of that for, each wheel
   a little clock face—

      circling, little whey-faced moon, button nose, cymbal, keeping
         time until
            face in its hands oh stop until

we come back for it—

II

I remember, the first time you left
—everything, then, was the first time—

226

overcome with the sheer
unlikeliness of it, and I said
        yes, okay, expecting nothing

        at all, and I sat on the step
and waited for you to
        return, like a child waiting
patiently after school, hoping
        that no one will notice

the shame of it. An hour passed, the wind
came up, just a little, as it was
        still summer, and after
a while I went inside and reset
        the clock of my life—east,

        south, north, west, the tick-tock
of our common life, in a minor city.
        I told myself, you are
not a child. Whatever
                that meant.

III   2 A.M.

and where do you think I'd got to?
skipped stone on the black water
skipped stone on the black water
stopped before I've started

as if it made no never mind
no one's business, no one's daughter

    give it a rest, why not?
A lowing cow is time
A red cock crowing is time

give it a rest, why not?

gone as the day is long
the whip-poor-will's song
    never make no never mind

       basilisk eye, star-archer,
       the orange moon knows me
       in its basket of branches

give it a rest, why not?
eye in the level
fit in a firkin
fly in the ointment

       Metis hammering

Minerva's cervelliere
      thumb-cap

listening for little owl's growl

listening for

       the jackdaw's rat-a-tat—
he'd rather starve than eat
    what he doesn't want,

Arachne
         under the camphor tree, the honeysuckle's
    dragooned green.

  Mine is the moon-face
     flipped coin

myself to myself   cold fish
   myself to myself

\

squirreled away in the hazel wood
   Oh, what will you give me

   says the new moon

lip staying the clapper
how long do we have

waiting
waiting

IV

What I wanted, I guess, was some sign,
   a slipper of light when the door opened
and moonlight slid silver on the yellow
floorboards, the yellow dark, almost muddy,
   stygian, in what were once called the small hours.
Why small, I wondered, when they seemed
      larger than the others, heavy with their cargo
         casting nervous shadows.

   So often, then, I stood
at the window, staring
      at the pitched rooftops
and sometimes the moon,

   what bit of it the sky
could muster, while love
      battered my heart, holding
a baby, or a telephone,

or resting my head in
my hands, each breath given
     over to the world's wide
wish, that we live until

    daybreak—the cat, the baby,
the blades of grass. These
     were hours from which I felt
I would never wake, although

from what I cannot say,
    as I never slept.

But in those shallows the hours were
small boats pulled up on the grassy shore,
sinking a little, then rising on the tide
as the rowers, one, or at most two, carried
packages to the wet bank, rice, or coffee,
a sheaf of letters. I wanted the hours
to float like dories on a pond choked
with lilies, where once long ago I drifted
with my book and you had your paints
and a small rose paint-spattered easel.
The midges rose in clouds. The water lilies,
white and lavender clung to the bottom
and though I tried pulling at their long stems
the bottom held them fast and the petals
    came off in my hands.

v

Which lost hour? The hour
I could not say your name, the hour
    I could?

Moonlight foams
    on its silver bridle,

and far off, the waves stitch
their lacework at the end
    of the jetty.

Here, over the Tiber, the gulls
    range like senators
in their grey and white suits,

the slim moon rises
    over the river,

the deserted
    stone haunts of the gods.

A hungry winter.

It is the same moon that rises
    hours later, over

your pine woods,

    the barn, the needle-nosed buildings,
the dog named beauty—

the moon you watch for, you who are always changing,

whose face I've known always,
    particulate but not yet defined,

changing and not changing, like a cat who doesn't
    care if we watch—

    your voice far off cataloguing

the diminishing hours, which

we understand now are the only ones

that stop for us and contain us—
        only this succession of moons,

the flower moon, the harvest moon,
        the blue moon and the pink one—

                and that our own shadows and reflections
                wavering on the mottled glassy lake,

meant less than
                the wheat and the grass, the ionized dusk—

the lost hour a can kicked down the dusty road
        into the cattails, lost, fetched again,

                cat up a tree, its emerald eyes
                        in the green leaves, if only—

and we remember how we imagined time
                could be restored if we searched for it,

because we believed in all the time in the world,

                and still, you turn to me saying, *this time.*

Next Day

The woodpile full of moths and mice,
wood turned to ash before it's lit ablaze—
at dawn, your dream, a mermaid

with a ticking fuse, slips through sleep's
bedraggled net, her whipsawed tail
a metronome.

What's to become of us?
A scant mile off, a tern, helter-skelter
at the low tide mark, writes its

question: *greater than, less than?* Sea foam
marbleizes each green wave, Neptune's
paradisiacal endpapers.

Last love,
the moth on fire, wings charred dun lavender
butts its velvet matchhead on the mantel.

If I love you less
let me be that gossamer.

Race Point

Fanfare of pipes, the clangor marking *home*—
    up too early, I settle old scores with myself,
each crossed-out loss a speaking chimera,

your cinquecento flower drawings,
    opening their mouths. Yesterday, the sand
violet, then aquamarine, the Coast Guard

turret a behemoth Bastet, cats'-eyes
    dim against dusk's lid of cloud cover.
But what's a compass with no compass rose?

Truro, Starksboro . . . the omphalos
    of old place names; the dog, trembling
at my feet, knows not to leave the car

for fear that she'll be left behind. Her remit—
    to love whomever touches her.

Farewell

So now again. At the harbor, the sun
goes down in tatters, like the end
of a terrible effort, and night unfurls
along the long drive back, draping
        the pines in darkness.

A long time ago and far away. From
the beginning I knew I would live
in corners, and I filled the house
with light, because it could not find
        me as the darkness could.

Now a sleek raven in the pine tree,
a black feather like a barbed fishbone.
    I haven't anything to give you,
nothing that time will not take away.

Four Poems to Astraeus

I   POMPEII

Presence of an absence, absence of a presence,
      which was it? Strings on a broken harp.
           How eager the earth is to have us in its debt—
dusk on loan from its library of hours.

At dawn our clattered knees are chariot wheels
      turning in the amber air, our numbered days
          a whizzing pinwheel zodiac: the sycamore,
the dog, the lobster trap, your long-dead mother's

tale of Pliny at Pompeii—grief, or madness
      to want the sky to fall and cover our blent
          bones with ash? This morning in New Haven
the bleached moon blotted by the rain, then light

      pressing its claim against the window, dawn
threading itself once more through time's needle.

II   THE HORNET'S NEST

A hut made of wood scraps and spit, fallen
or hacked, planetary, as if a cat
      had licked a kitten clean, dropped underfoot

      where the leaves are gold in the dry woods;
an inch or so off, the limping hornet
      thumb-sized, a tiny yellow roadster, red

leather monkey-face abroad in autumn's
galaxy of loss. Tonight the moon
    mother-of-pearl on dusk's rent cloak; numinous,

    the candelabra of the locust tree
stung with pink and gold light. Our wrongs ring
    changes, walk the boards—once, I thought, in that

    first intake of breath, this cannot hurt me
  —love my witness to the world's imprecations.

III   TO ASTRAEUS

Pale blue, the split days pure radium,
    bittersweet lace in the snow-white field,
    the red seeds ladybirds, gold husks papyrus,

the fine print reading, *fly away home.*
    But we are home. Morose, angelic
    your dirigibles flap their glassine wings

above the pond, the ice boat's matchbox
    traps ignite their peacock halos. Our smoky
    offerings provoke, not please—even

the green-gold coverlet, its diamond
    panes unstitched, shifts from us off the bed.
    Live here with me? Twilight's inamorati

smudge the lawn. From the ceiling you look down,
    holding Eros' dumbstruck thunderbolt.

Life asks us for so little we can bear—
    my wrinkled hand on the pillow, a goose beak,
  the clouds, your twin silos, mother and father

dumb in the gray-green-gold light, the children's
    emissaries from the land of the dead,
  flying ghosts under the eaves, like shuttlecocks.

Brambles lacerate the broken lintel.
    The risorgimento teeters, regains ground,
  your reading glasses bull's-eyes for the sun's

jackknife spyglass, the bullied bittersweet
    snapping back under day's sloping ceiling—
  the tamped-down ground where once we stood upright.

    Love draws us with its eyes closed.
      Whatever happens . . . but it has happened.

November

Nine swallows on the stripped beech tree,
the ragged leaves on the topmost branch
        just holding on,

bruised clouds swarming
      over the rutted field,
                day almost/finished but

for a smear of blue near the ridge,
      dusk's smoke stains
    smiting the stiff fingers of the cattails.

        Night's black bell settles
on the shut house, the brindle-
   backed hedge.

       Because I knew
I was meant for loneliness,
      you were whom I chose to love: ghost, pursuer—

both of us caught in a dream.
      One day you came with a load
of kindling, each twig encased in ice.

     Or was that also a dream, that too—

I know you never meant to do me harm,
   the swallows jet on my bare arms.

Gare du Nord

Pale silk spilling from a tortoise shell clip
   crow black sleeve reaching for the overhead rack—
     and there we are, a lifetime ago
on Pierrepont Street, caramel hair gold leaf on your
     black coat, the river smell seaweed and tarmac,
         the curb

wet after rain and all of us soaked
    to the bone, the children singing *fa so la.*
     In the station, the train's headlight
a spirit lamp, a silver brooch of stalactites, the car
     the long boat over the black water
         an oar

splitting the Lagoon. Hot tea. Archangelsk. The splintered
    snowbound road. After all these years
       I've forgotten how to write to you.
And that red smear on your hand? Lily pollen, the handkerchief
    petals white in the station's
         anthracite air.

Call me when you get there, you said. All right then—
    I'm doing as you asked, and calling
       across the pleated water, from this place you knew
always, beaded with ash and sorrow. Or at least
    as you would say, making
         another try—

Notes

FIRE LYRIC

"Learning German": The first line quoted in section one is from "The Waste Land" by T. S. Eliot and first appears in *Tristan und Isolde* by Richard Wagner; the second is from *Duino Elegies* by Rainer Maria Rilke.

THE ADA POEMS

Throughout the text, quotes from *Ada, or Ardor: A Family Chronicle* by Vladimir Nabokov (McGraw-Hill, 1969) are represented by italics within quotation marks.

"Birch": The phrase quoted is from *Absalom, Absalom* by William Faulkner (New York: Random House, 1936).

"Third Dreamscape": The scene on the stairway in this section's final stanza appears in a novel by William Maxwell, *The Château* (New York: Alfred A. Knopf, 1961).

ORBIT

"Rainy Day Fugue": The quote in the poem's second section is from *The Bostonians* by Henry James (1886).

"The Impulse Wants Company" and "Dear and Blackbirds" were commissioned by BalletCollective. Ballets based on these poems (choreography by Troy Schumacher, music by Ellis Ludwig-Leone) premiered in New York City on August 14, 2013, and October 18, 2014, respectively.

The following poems have been set for music and voice: "Round for a Plague Year" (*The Watercourse*) by Ted Rosenthal; "Port Imperial" (*The Watercourse*) by Massimo Nunzi; "Monday Rhyme (Khartoum)" (*The Ada Poems*), "Flowers" and "Blue Vase" (*Orbit*), and "Marina" (*Next Day*) by Eric Schorr.

Acknowledgments

The new poems in this volume first appeared in the following publications: "Marina," "Next Day," "April," "Pompeii," "To Astraeus," "Gare du Nord," and "November" in *The New Yorker;* "At Putney" in *The New York Review of Books;* "Autumnal" in *The Times Literary Supplement;* "Race Point" and "Farewell" in *The Yale Review;* and "The Lost Hour" in *Raritan.* "Hornet's Nest" first appeared in *Il Fatto Quotidiano,* as "Nido di Vespe," translated by Stella Sacchini. "After Anna Akhmatova" was published by the Academy of American Poets in the Poem-a-Day series and in Italian as part of a performance piece, "Women Poets Against Tyranny," Venice, 2018.

Thanks are due to the MacDowell Colony, the Corporation of Yaddo, La Devignere, and the American Academy in Rome. For help with the compilation of this volume, to Owen Andrews; at Alfred A. Knopf, to Deborah Garrison, incomparable editor and friend; and to the late Harry and Kathleen Ford. And to my children, Anna, Rose, Jack, and Beatrice.

Index of Titles

A NOTE ABOUT THE AUTHOR

Cynthia Zarin was born in New York City and educated at Harvard and Columbia. She is the author of five previous collections, including, most recently, *Orbit;* a novel, *Inverno;* two books of essays, *Two Cities* and *An Enlarged Heart;* and several books for children. She is a longtime contributor to *The New Yorker* and the recipient of fellowships from the Guggenheim Foundation, the National Endowment for the Arts, and the Ingram Merrill Foundation. A winner of the Peter I. B. Lavan Younger Poets Award and the Los Angeles Times Book Prize, she teaches at Yale and lives in New York City.

A NOTE ON THE TYPE

This book was set in Adobe Garamond. Designed for the Adobe Corporation by Robert Slimbach, the fonts are based on types first cut by Claude Garamond (ca. 1480–1561). Garamond was a pupil of Geoffroy Tory and is believed to have followed the Venetian models, although he introduced a number of important differences, and it is to him that we owe the letters we now know as "old style." He gave to his letters a certain elegance and feeling of movement that won their creator an immediate reputation and the patronage of Francis I of France.

Composed by North Market Street Graphics
Lancaster, Pennsylvania

Printed and bound by Berryville Graphics
Berryville, Virginia

Book design by Pei Loi Koay